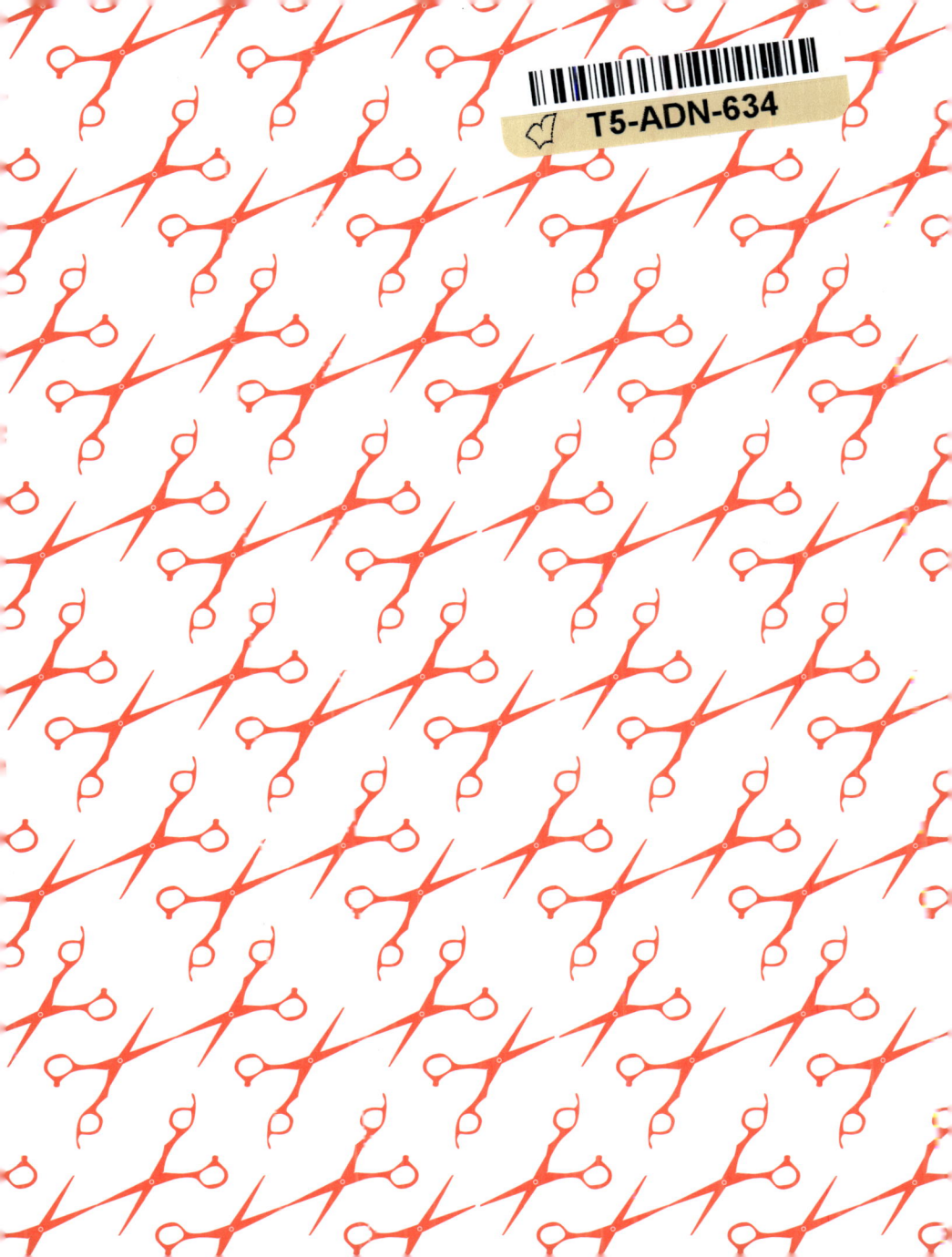

cut it out

RECREATE YOUR FAVORITE DICTATOR'S HAIRSTYLE AT HOME – FOR FUN AND PROFIT!

Bryan "The Brush" Burnsides

GRAND CENTRAL PUBLISHING

NEW YORK   BOSTON

Text copyright © 2018 by Tom Henry and Pencil On The Shark Productions

Illustrations copyright © 2017 by Jed Franklin

Cover copyright © 2018 by Hachette Book Group, Inc.

Hachette Book Group supports the right to free expression and the value of copyright. The purpose of copyright is to encourage writers and artists to produce the creative works that enrich our culture.

The scanning, uploading, and distribution of this book without permission is a theft of the author's intellectual property. If you would like permission to use material from the book (other than for review purposes), please contact permissions@hbgusa.com. Thank you for your support of the author's rights.

Grand Central Publishing
Hachette Book Group
1290 Avenue of the Americas, New York, NY 10104
grandcentralpublishing.com
twitter.com/grandcentralpub

First published in Great Britain in 2017 by Constable
First U.S. Edition: March 2018

Grand Central Publishing is a division of Hachette Book Group, Inc. The Grand Central Publishing name and logo is a trademark of Hachette Book Group, Inc.

The publisher is not responsible for websites (or their content) that are not owned by the publisher.

The Hachette Speakers Bureau provides a wide range of authors for speaking events. To find out more, go to www.hachettespeakersbureau.com or call (866) 376-6591.

Photo credits can be found on page 91

Print book interior design by Sian Rance and Emil Dacanay at D. R. ink

ISBNs: 978-1-5387-1242-9 (paper over board), 978-1-5387-1241-2 (ebook)

Printed in the United States of America

PHX

10 9 8 7 6 5 4 3 2 1

Believe it or not, it takes more than megalomania, ruthlessness and homicidal tendencies to create a dictator.

In fact, it's all in the hair!

After years of investigation, celebrity stylist Bryan 'The Brush' Burnsides reveals how every badass in history has climbed the pole of power on the back of the most radical 'dos the world has ever seen. Science now proves that 'the badder the dude, the bigger the 'do' and in this book we feature looks that will send you ballistic and have you running to your nearest salon to rock those locks.

'The Brush' brings years of salon experience to this fascinating study of nifty trims for nasty guys and gals. For the first time, he shows how the original 'dos were done and shares the trade secrets of the underground stylists of today, hell-bent on creating total retro-hair war!

So, dust off the Mao suit, slip on an armband and get ready for Big Bad Hair!

kim jong-un

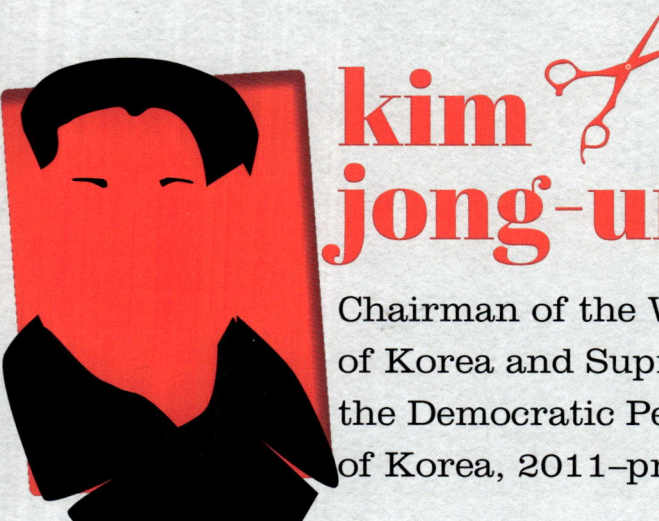

Chairman of the Workers' Party of Korea and Supreme Leader of the Democratic People's Republic of Korea, 2011–present

For Kim Jong-un, read Kim Wrong-un. Wow . . . the fat North Korean superbrat has the badass 'do to end all badass 'dos. Truly, only crazy Kim could rock a crop that resembles a matador's hat atop a brontosaurus egg.

An early obsession with Disneyland and Mickey Mouse is thought to have inspired Kim's unique style. The wearing of comedy mouse ears on parade was discouraged by Kim's father, the late Kim Jong-il, and a not-so-subtle act of rebellion in a downtown Pyongyang barber's followed.

When Kim Snr died, his son invested billions in secret shipments of hair-clipping devices. The reason for this was revealed when Kim Jnr decreed that every male in North Korea should sport his look – or risk becoming the mystery ingredient in dog soup, the nation's favourite dish. This quickly ensured the cut's enduring popularity.

For sure, it's a statement haircut. And if we're about anything here at Brush Barber's, we're all about statements. Kim's cut features a deeper-than-a-missile-silo shade of black and has echoes of the Herr 'Hair' Hitler with a kooky Oriental twist that will keep heads turning long after yours has dropped into the guillotine basket.

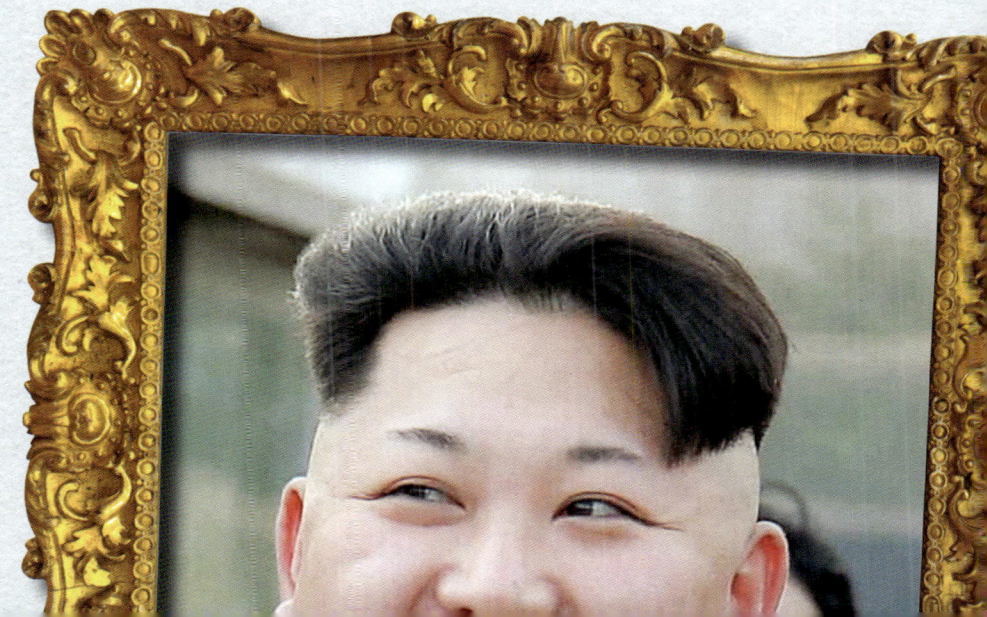

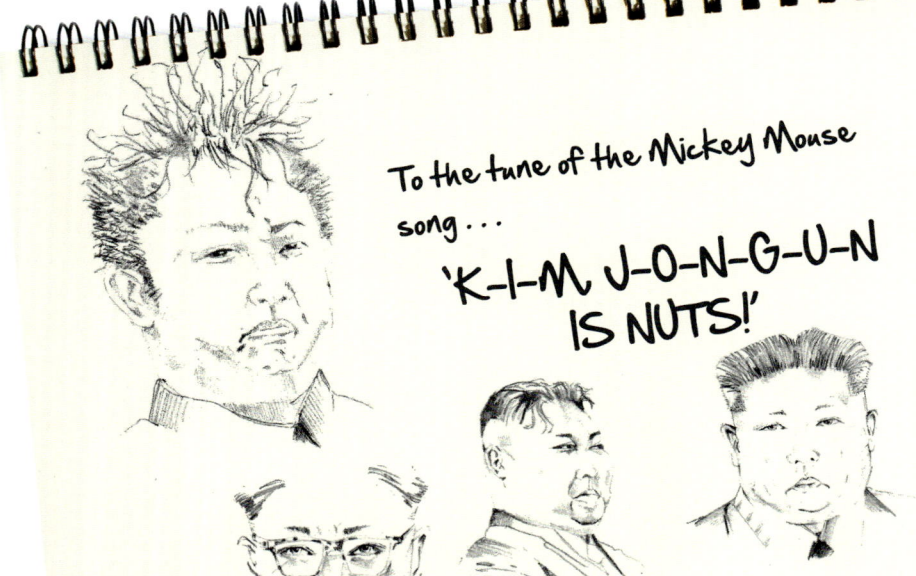

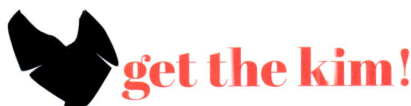
get the kim!

1) Gently tease the tresses away from the ears and use clippers on a Number One setting to shave a strip two inches wide from ear upwards.

2) Using a curling wand, take the front of the cut up towards the crown, and into a tsunami flick. Lube with a combination of my own Trans-Man styling wax and a palmful of plutonium.

3) Next, razor the remainder of the strip and the back of the neck with a steady hand. If you're barbering a tubby North Korean, take care not to to nick your client's jugular – remember, he has your whole family tied to a ballistic missile.

4) Snake the fringe (front right side) slightly towards the left eye before teasing the whole 'do into the classic 'Matador' / 'Mouse ears' shape.

grigori rasputin

Spiritual Adviser to the Imperial Russian court, 1906–1916

In the words of the incomparable Boney M, Grigori Rasputin was 'Russia's greatest love machine', even in the days of horse and cart. And based on his lumbersexual hipster looks, he was no stranger to the flat white either.

Had he been alive today, Ras would've loved nothing better than riding his fixie around Moscow, checking out wood-fired sourdough pizzerias and using FaceTime to inflict disturbing poetry on pale, interesting girls. His beardy charms wooed no less than the Czarina herself, and it's that bristle-brush look which is inspiring a whole generation of puny snowflakes to man up and Go East.

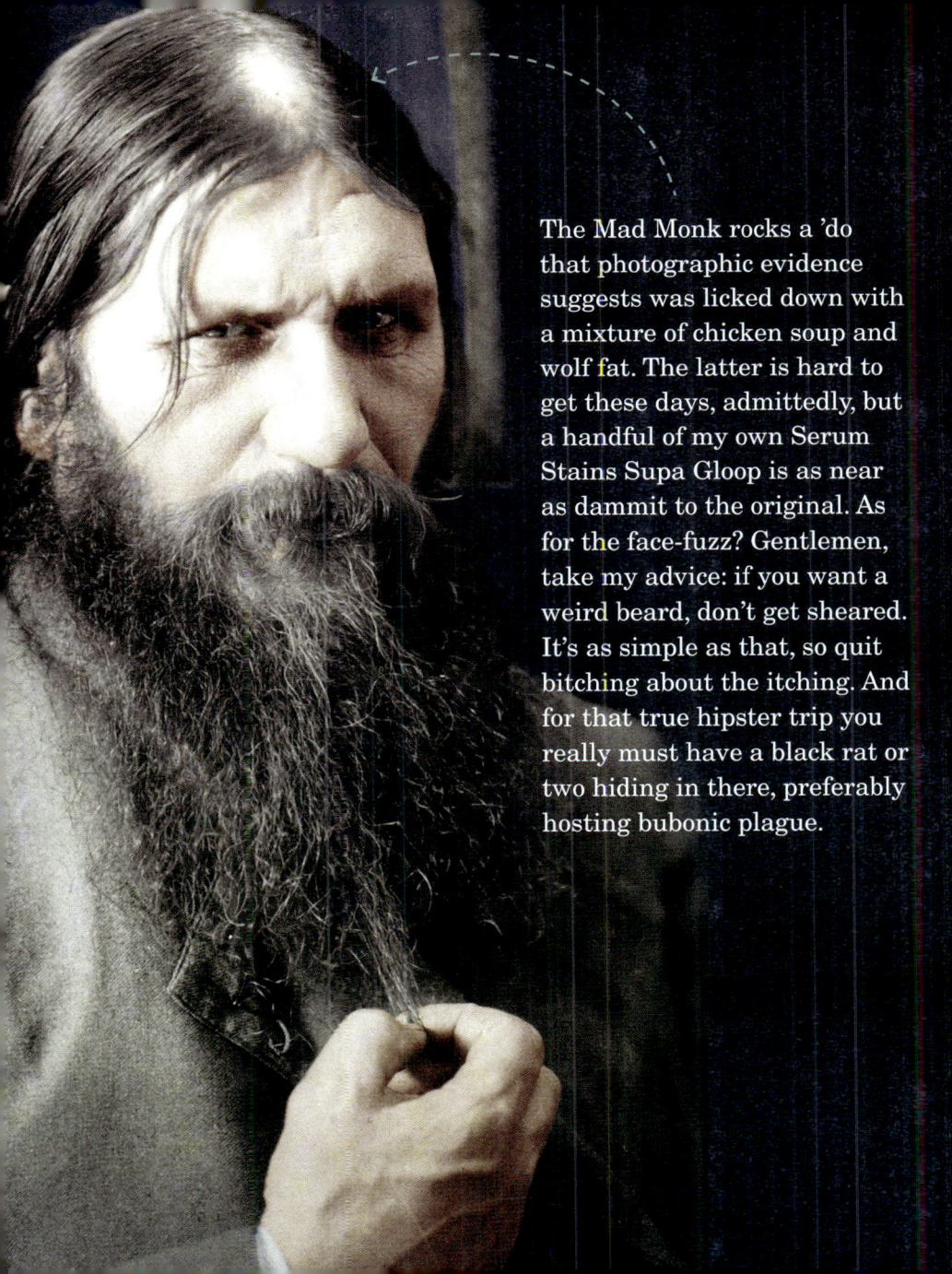

The Mad Monk rocks a 'do that photographic evidence suggests was licked down with a mixture of chicken soup and wolf fat. The latter is hard to get these days, admittedly, but a handful of my own Serum Stains Supa Gloop is as near as dammit to the original. As for the face-fuzz? Gentlemen, take my advice: if you want a weird beard, don't get sheared. It's as simple as that, so quit bitching about the itching. And for that true hipster trip you really must have a black rat or two hiding in there, preferably hosting bubonic plague.

Ra-Ra-Ras
what a hip priest he is!

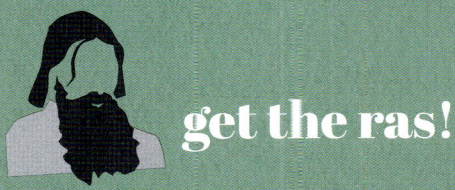

get the ras!

1) Use Made For Monks Super Serious ash-grey volumiser to work that badger-stripe along the centre parting, then rub the hair vigorously and frequently with discarded chicken wings and wolf fat (or The Brush's Serum Stains Supa Gloop if you don't have access to wolves).

2) Pull up the man-bun and trim any spare locks to collar length. DO NOT cut evenly – we're talking chewed ends here.

3) The beard. Let it grow, grow, grow! But keep it sharp with a cut-throat. Accessorise with an icon, or the fingerbones of a child saint. Think rad, think religion!

4) Match the total look with a tunic of mortifying sackcloth, then pussycat those Romanovs with a major piercing stare.

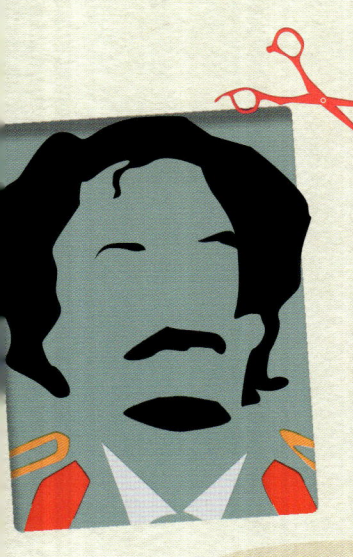

muammar 'colonel' gaddafi

Revolutionary Chairman of the Libyan Arab Republic, 1969–2011

In his later years he resembled something plucked from a palm tree and left to shrivel in the midday sun, but Google Colonel Muammar Gaddafi in his 70s and 80s prime and you'll see why they called him 'The Shit of the Desert': his appeal to otherwise incorruptible maidens was total.

In a word, Gadders was HOT – and not just under that crazy kaftan. In a natty green army suit and sporting an Omar Sharif-style blow-wave, the Colonel was every inch the Hollywood matinee idol, complete with chiselled cheekbones and come-to-Bedouin eyes.

But Time is a cruel mistress. Fast forward 30 years and Gaddafi is stripping the nation's oil reserve – and applying most of it to his curly locks – quicker than you can say 'terrorist arms shipment'.

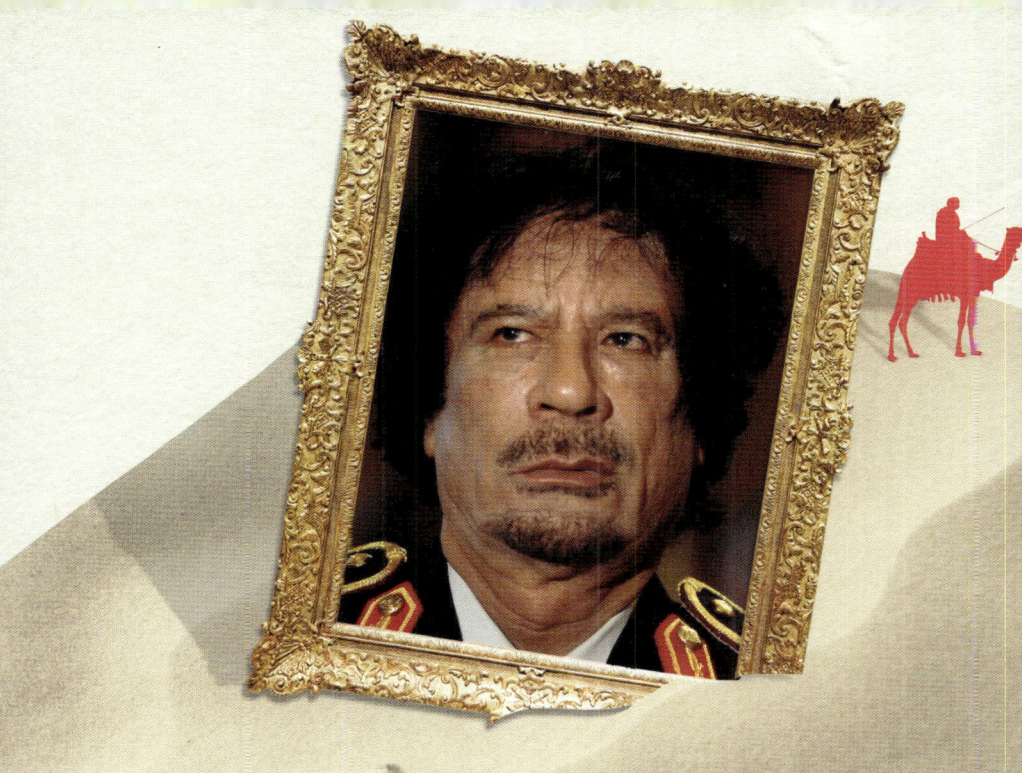

And this from a man who had the world's only coterie of female bodyguards. Didn't those girlfriends think about giving him a hefty hint, or were they too busy lying around the pool, semi-clad and gyrating slowly to the sound of gentle lapping?

The 2011 Arab Spring didn't work out too well for Gadders. His 'Top Gun'-style mirrored shades reflected plenty of uncomfortable truths he didn't care to address. But even as the lynch mob grabbed him and he rolled dead into a ditch, that killer 'Thriller' Wacko-Jacko bubble perm hung on stubbornly. The Colonel was a Grade A badass, but boy, did he know how to work product . . .

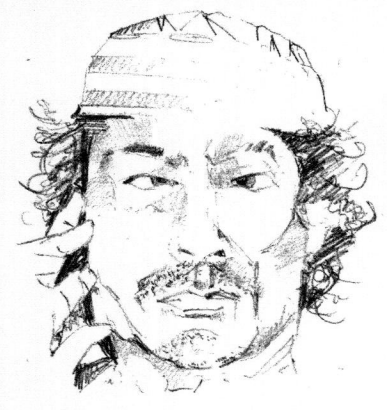
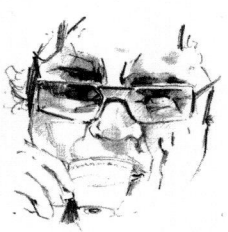
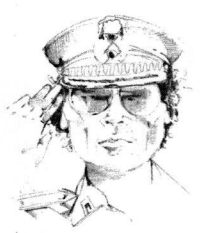

Like the Wet Look never went away!

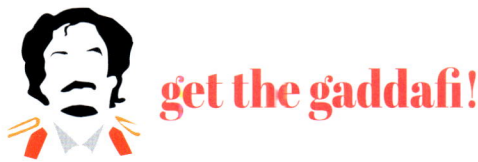

get the gaddafi!

1) Expose yourself to sand. Lots of sand, until it gets in your eyes and makes them very weird indeed.

2) Clip according to mood, and against trend. It's the late 60s, and every dude looks like Jesus. OK, so you go short, sleek, sharp. Now it's the 80s, and everyone's gone curly-whirly. You too!

3) Take tea. Lots of tea. Keeps you cool, if you needed to be any cooler.

4) LAPD shades and a natty hat complement those cheekbones beautifully. You are the Shit Of The Desert!

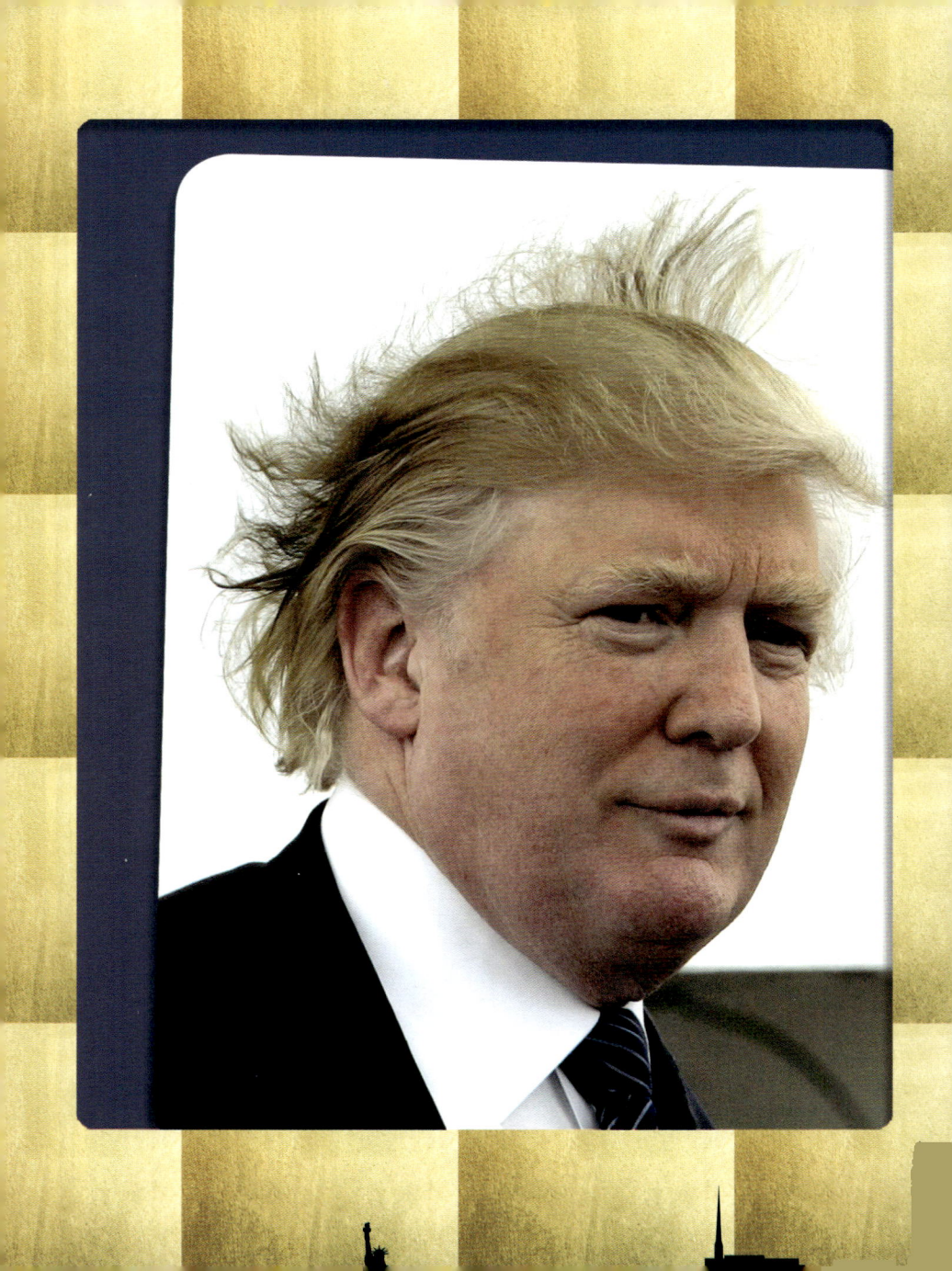

donald trump

45th President of the United States, 2017–present

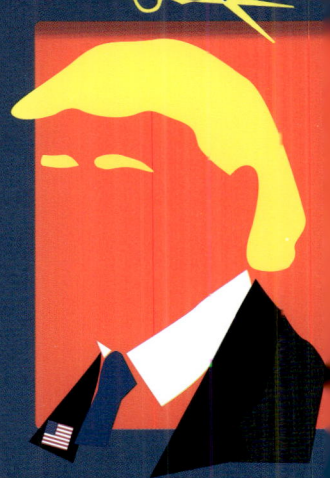

New York City, 1986. In a gilded skyscraper bearing your name, 68 storeys above Fifth Avenue, you're seconds into a private screening of steamy eroto-drama *Nine and a Half Weeks*. Suddenly, the screen is filled with the luscious Kim Basinger, her honeyed tresses framing lips bee-stung to perfection. You are blown away. 'Beautiful . . .' you whisper, 'such a beautiful 'do. And when I'm President, I too will pout and preen just like you, bitch.'

Fast forward three decades. As you receive the Seals of Office on a cold January day, a whisper of wind threatens the existence of the gilded Pacific roller now crowning your head. Instinctively, you pull your mouth into the famous constipated goldfish shape, and the wind bows before you. You are the Master of the Universe. And your hair is the Master of Alternative Facts.

The Donald and The Donald's hair have been making news for decades, of course, but now, after a Senate inquiry, His Master's claim that his aerodynamic thatch is spun from 22-carat gold thread by a team of former Miss Worlds looks decidedly uncertain. Still, as 'dos go, this is a design classic. The question is: will it remain in position for two whole terms? And what really did happen to all those missing cats around 57th and Fifth?

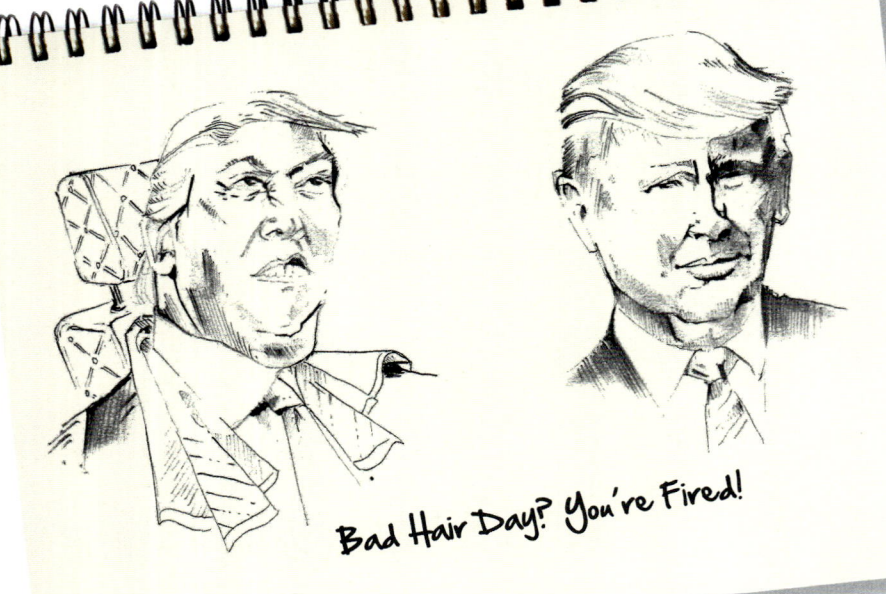

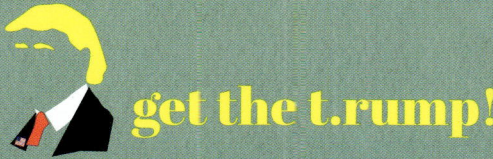# get the t.rump!

1) Using a heavy-duty detangle brush, sweep the existing hair forwards and across, and into a surfboard shape. Drop the 80s stubble, LOSER!

2) Blend a pinch of monosodium glutamate with lactic acid, citric acid and artificial colouring (Canary Yellow), then spray liberally upwards to achieve the desired 'Cheetos' shade.

3) Use moulding wax, or my own-brand 'KKK Pointy Head' styling gel, to fix the hair firmly, then bring any non-white strands into line by threatening them with expulsion.

4) With strong glue, and a thin tissue of untruths, stick the whole 'do onto the top of the head.

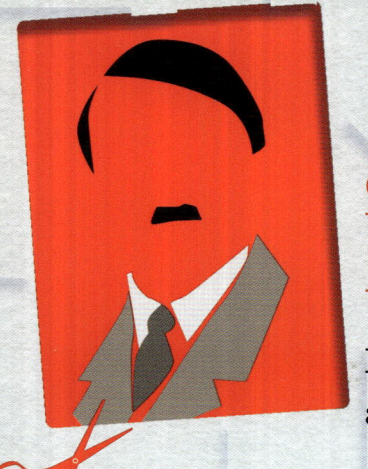

adolf hitler

Führer of the German Realm and People, 1934–1945

At what point did talentless twenty-something artist and World War One veteran Adolf Hitler think, 'You see this handlebar moustache? Wouldn't it be a great idea to trim it into the size and shape of a postage stamp and goose-step around Berlin like a demented Charlie Chaplin?'

History doesn't record the exact moment, but it's clear that it was pivotal; in a few short years that little black shadow under his nose helped transform antsy Adders into the Supreme Führer of all Germany (and a few other places besides). OK, by 1945 things weren't looking great, leading to an altercation with a revolver in the bunker, but up to that point Adolf 'Hot-ler' had mesmerised his nation to the point of obsession.

Decades on, the short-back-and-shaved-sides haircut is still popular among the disgruntled and dysfunctional. But what of the moustache? Despite attempts (see 'Robert Mugabe') the Toothbrush has never found widespread popularity again. Which is sad, really, because its streamlined looks do not allow crumbs to stick to it, enhancing your rant to the Reichstag, and it's also extremely handy for a 'Legends of Hollywood' theme party.

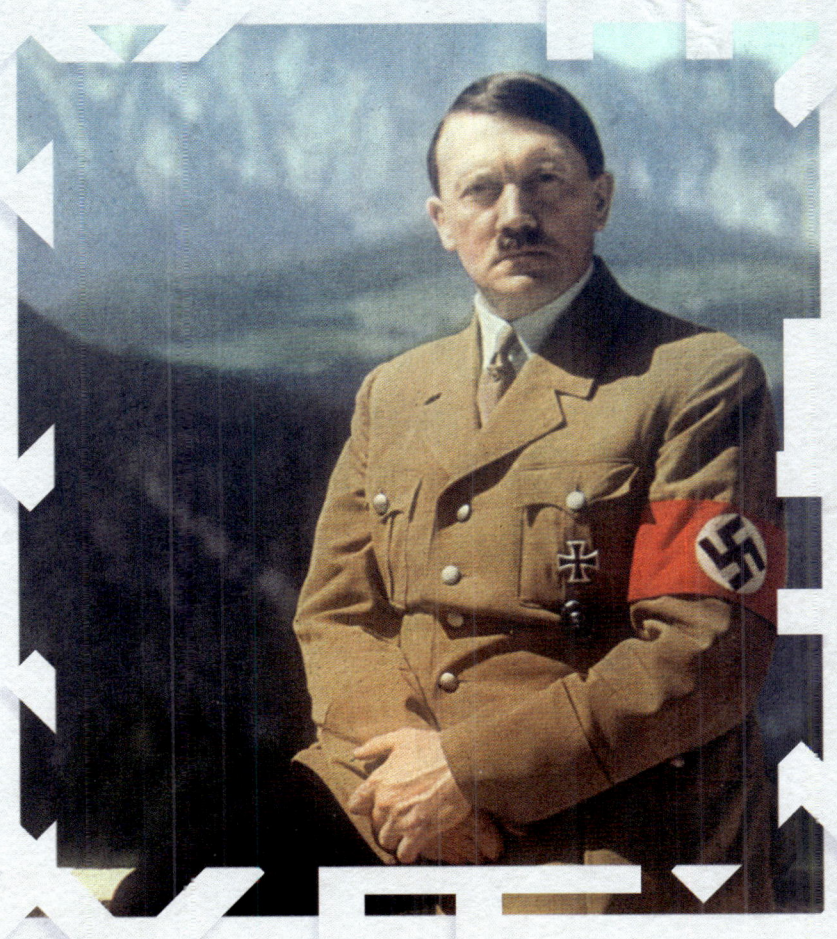

But if we're about anything at Brush Barbers, we're about counter-intuition. The Herr 'Hair' Hitler is a real Führer-cracker of a 'dare-to' look, and is great in shades other than Nightmare Black. Match a blue Toothbrush with a natty blazer and rakish yachting cap, or go for Green and help expand Adolf's cool vision for a vegetarian future. And don't forget the matching swastika armband – after all, it's only an ancient Hindu symbol!

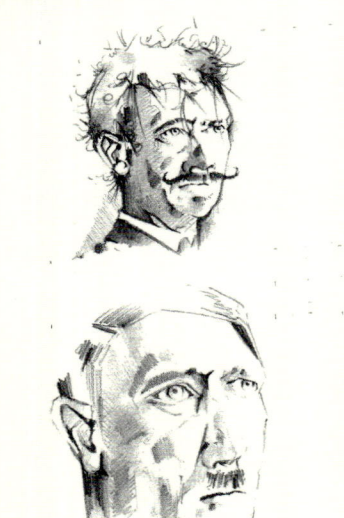
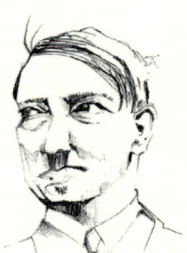
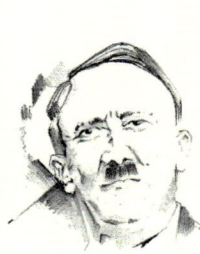

From Poorer to Phew-rer! Sieg Heil – let's go!!

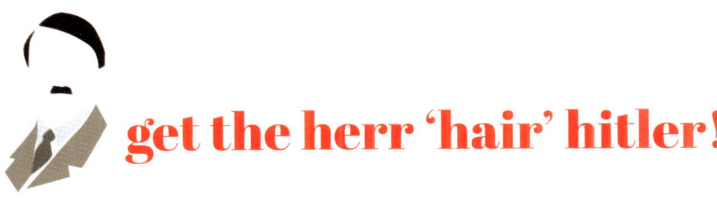

get the herr 'hair' hitler!

1) Pull yourself together, get out of the garbage can and have a darned good wash, a decent haircut and a reduction of your dumpster face-fuzz to a tip-top Toothbrush.

2) Stare maniacally at your barber in the mirror as his trembling hands give the sides of your head a Number One clipper cut all round.

3) Order that a lick of my Not-Tested-On-Alsatian-Dogs hair oil be applied before the side-parting is made in one highly efficient sweep.

4) Using a little extra grease, make sure several strands of hair are allowed to swing freely, especially in the middle of a hate-filled rant.

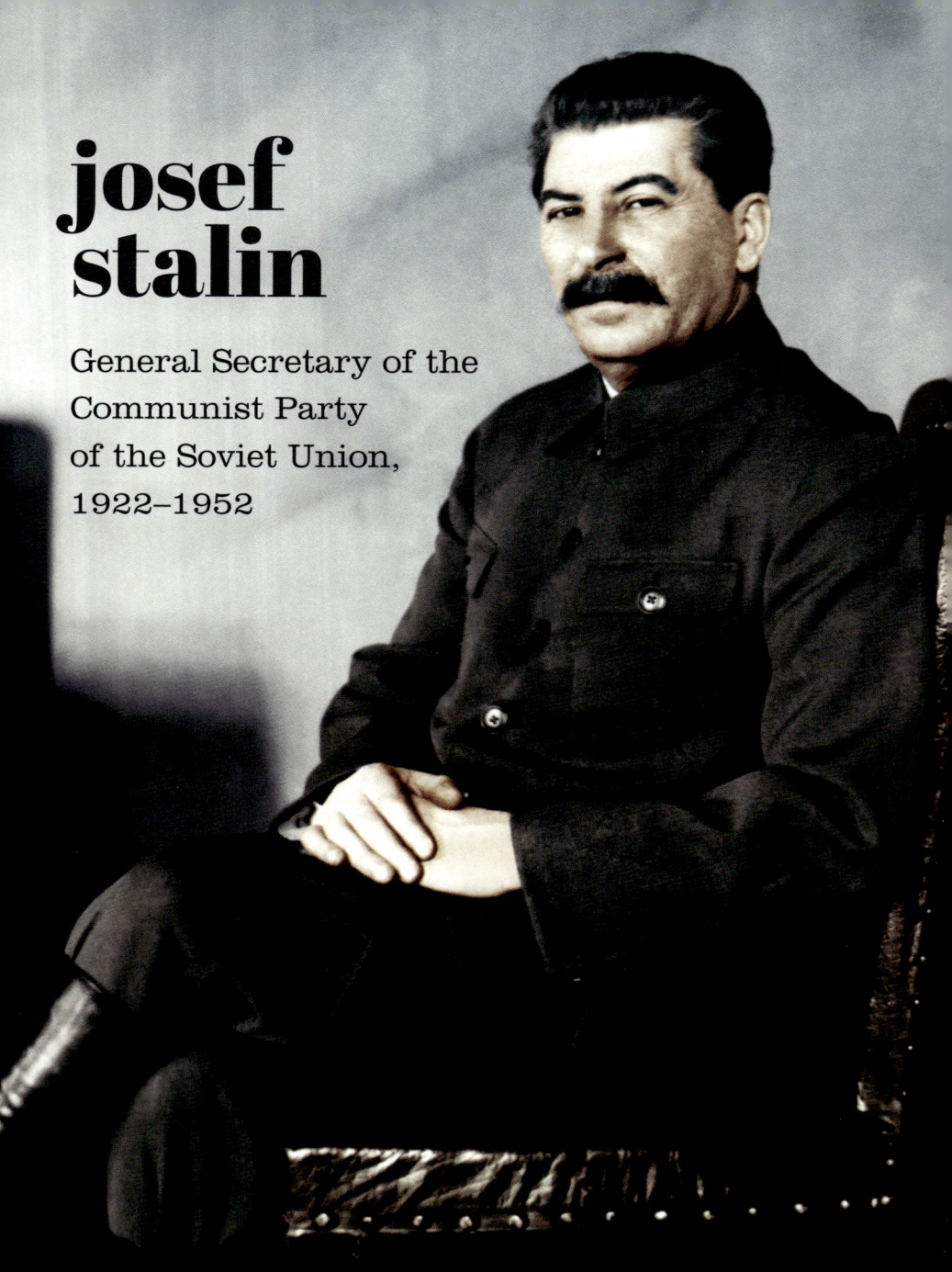

josef stalin

General Secretary of the Communist Party of the Soviet Union, 1922–1952

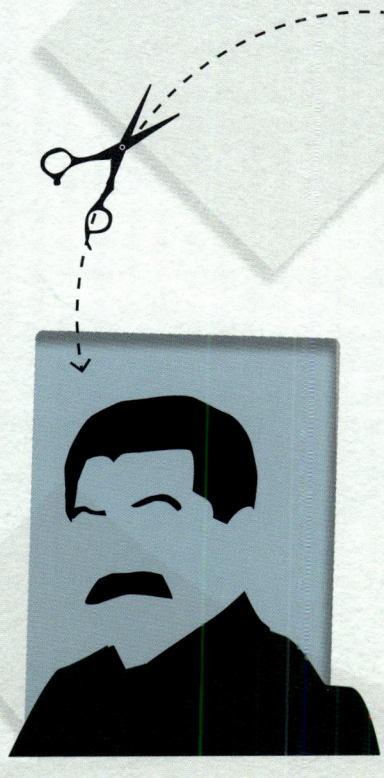

War, famine, terror, siege, repression, purges, gulags – 'Uncle Joe' Stalin presided over all this and more, and still had time to carefully tend his luxuriant bouffant and impressive 'silent movie villain' moustache. Quite a guy, huh?

From his early beginnings as a poet and journalist, Stalin cultivated a rakish, devil-may-care look at odds with his black heart. Years later, and now Supreme Leader of the USSR, the 'Man of Steel' is said to have used a specially designed domestic fork to keep his salt-and-pepper semi-wave in perfect symmetry.

Slowly, the Stalin style began to spread. In Memphis, Tennessee, a young Elvis Presley saw footage of Uncle Joe inspecting a chicken collective and, bowled over by the bouffant, began to sweep up his own thatch, thereby rewriting rock'n'roll history.

Today, the Stalin Sweep is a staple of men's hairdressing; the moustache a little less so. However, connoisseurs of tyrants' facial hair will know that to complete the lesson in evil, a short twist should be given to each end of the mo'. Complete the look with a cat on your knee and add a coterie of cowering lackeys.

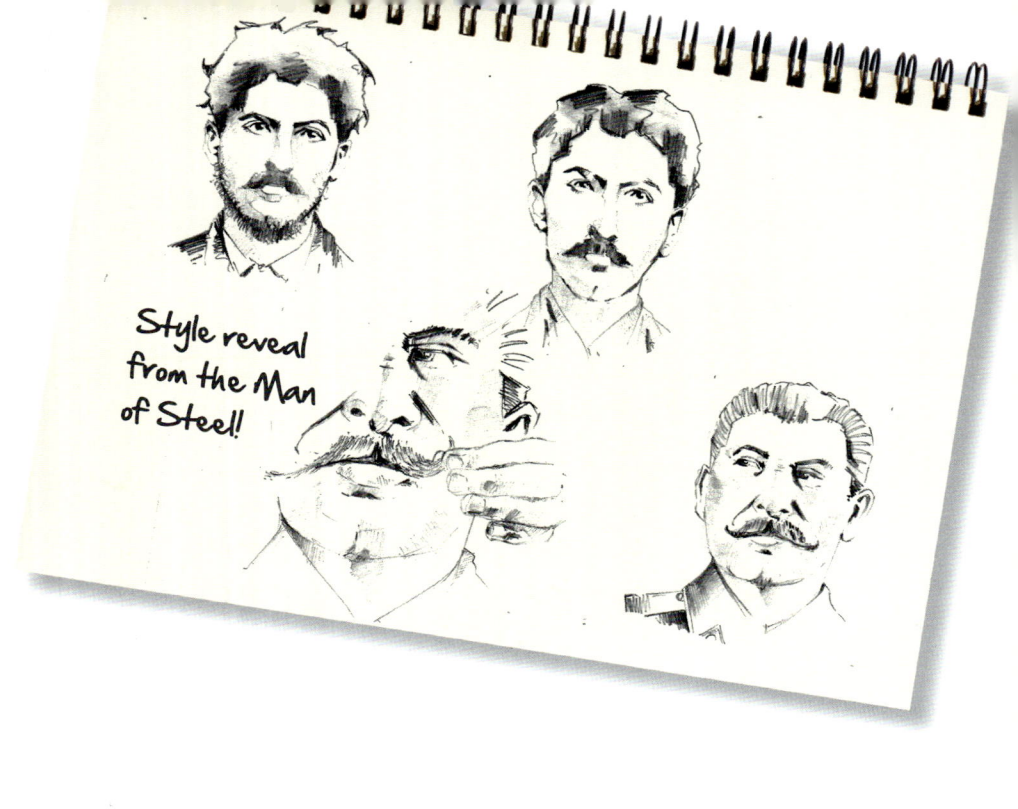

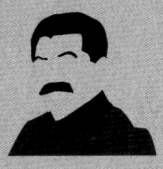 **get the stalin-grand!**

1) Shave the sad-ass student beard, leaving a fulsome handlebar moustache.

2) With a bone-handled fork of your choice, sweep back the hair and exile any stray strands to a very far-off place.

3) With a small drop of wax, carefully style the ends of the moustache into little points.

4) Twirl these ends thoughtfully at regular intervals, and notice how unsettled your friends and family become.

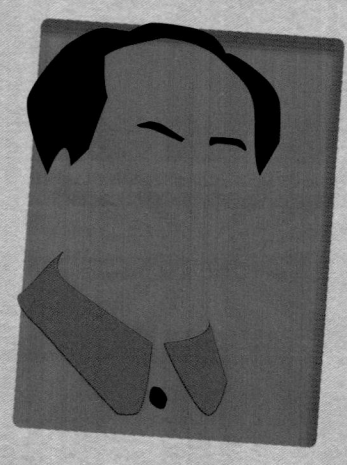

mao tse-tung

1st Chairman of the Communist Party of China, 1945–1976

When he wasn't taking great leaps forward or organising mass sparrow shootings, Chairman Mao loved nothing better than persuading his loyal subjects to wear his favourite garment, a Beatles suit. That the young Beatles were still in their strollers when this decree was issued is, of course, Fake News (see The T-Rump).

Mr Tse-tung's unlikely emulation of what would become the world's most popular singing group did not extend to his hair. Try as he might, he could not grow the famed 'Mop Top' in sufficient quantity to cover his head. It's sad to report that his thatch was actually taking a Great Leap Backwards – right off the top of his dome.

Naturally, this led to a dilemma: would the Communist Emperor continue his pursuit of Liverpudlian locks, or shave off the whole thing? After much debate within the Forbidden City a compromise was reached. The Chairman would go all Fab around the back and sides and leave the frontage high and smooth. A 30-minute standing ovation accompanied this decree but sadly, the resulting 'do was more plumptious potted-meat salesman than pretty Paul McCartney. Though no one dared say that at the time.

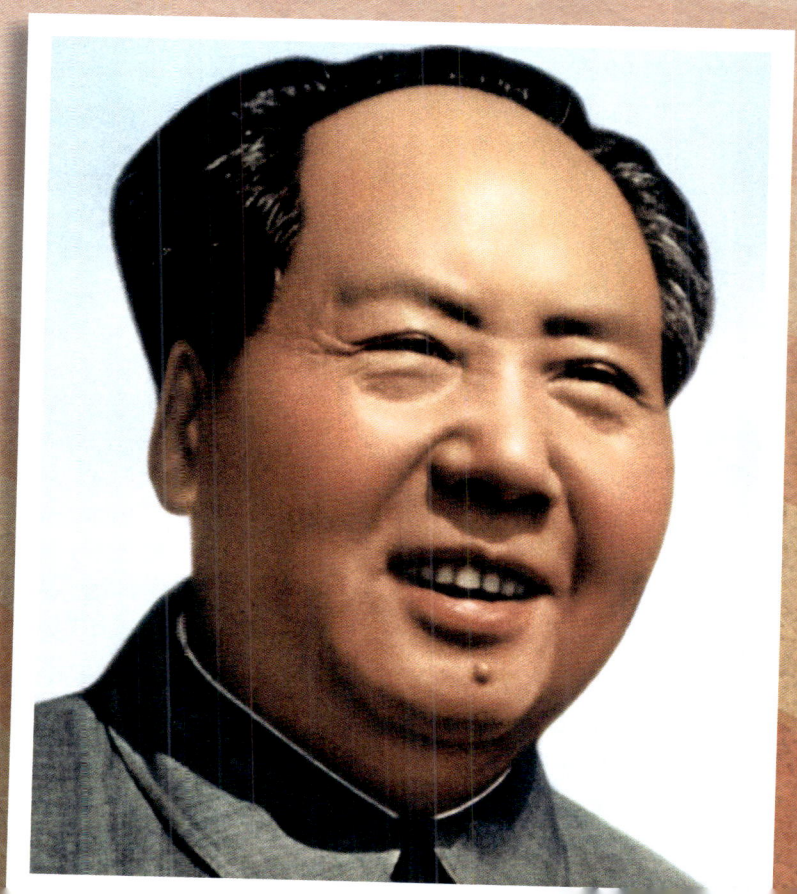

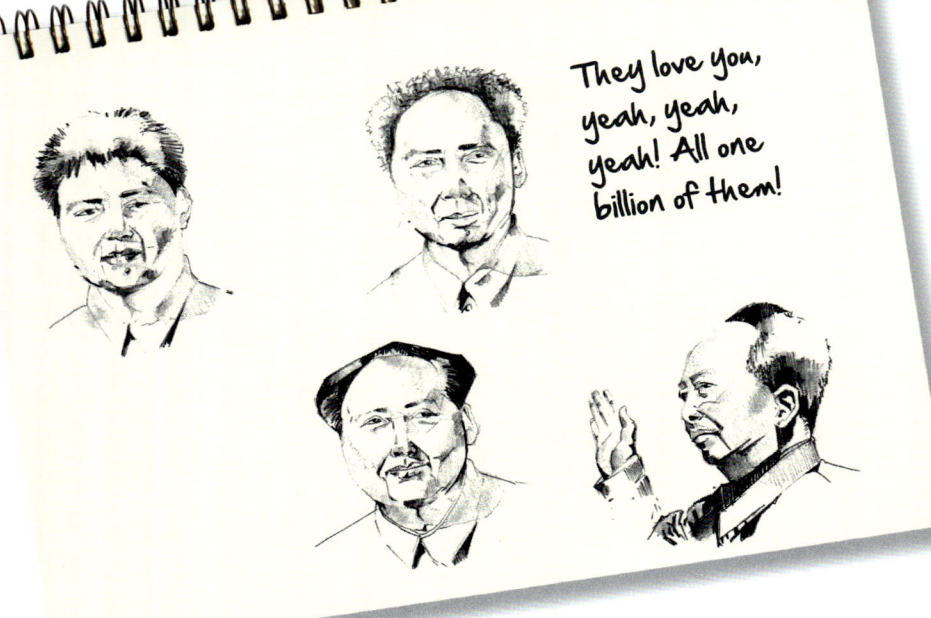

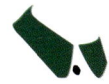

get the mao-mop!

1) Using an open razor, shave the front of the hair into a half-moon extending just below the crown.

2) Now, using The Little Red Book of Topiary as a source, sculpt the sides high, and into 'ears'.

3) Next, eat your own body weight in wontons until you have reached the right level of plumptiousness.

4) Smile broadly, wave at any passing missiles and ignore the baleful stares of the sparrow population.

idi amin dada

3rd President of Uganda, 1971–1979

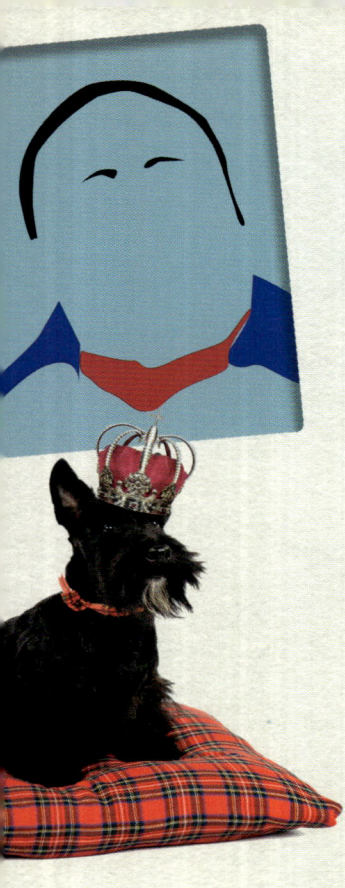

Guys, we're all worried about our masculinity these days, huh? All this gender fluidity, 'trans' this, 'trans' that – it's a tough world for a real man. A quick look at former Ugandan dictatomonster (and suspected cannibal) Idi Amin's biog reveals that the identity crisis we face today is nothing new – imagine waking up one morning and declaring yourself King of Scotland.

That's what General Amin did, and to prove his credentials he had his hair cropped close in order that a series of natty Glengarry and Tam O'Shanter hats (fake ginger thatch not included) fitted better on his befuddled head. He was already self-declared Lord of All the Beasts of the Earth and Fishes of the Seas, of course, but that role didn't come with such nice headgear.

In truth, Idi's hair was the most nondescript thing about him and yet its banality served a vital role, that of not deflecting attention away from his manly chest and the vast array of medals upon it (including the British Victoria Cross) that he kindly awarded himself. Which all goes to prove, if you want to get ahead, get a hat, if you want to get a hat, get a head!

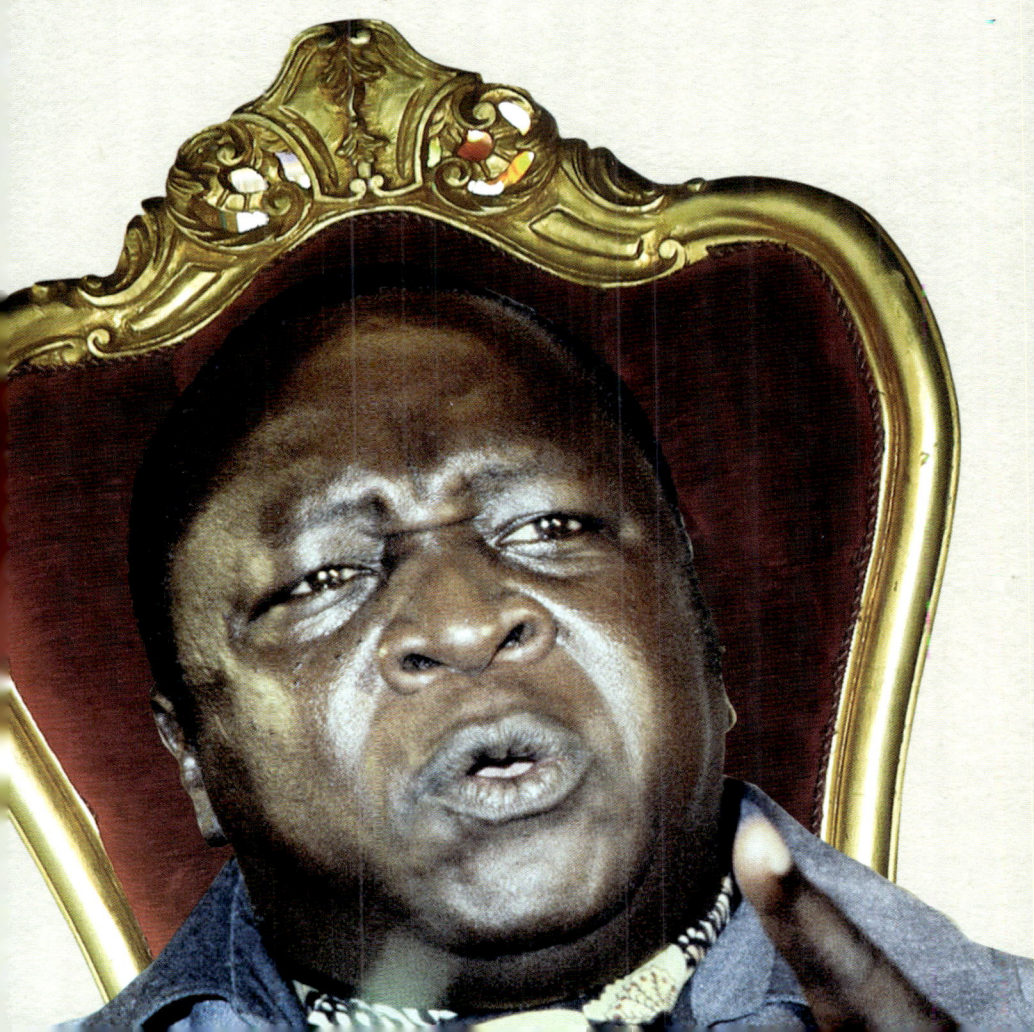

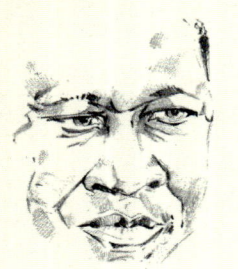
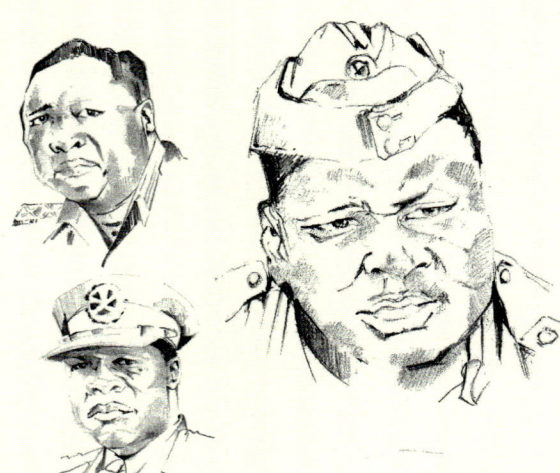

Does my kilt look big in this?!

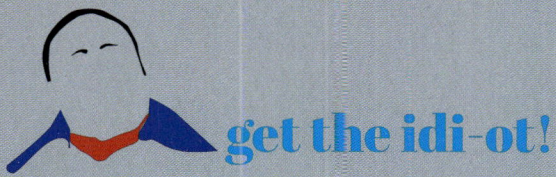# get the idi-ot!

1) Scissor then razor the hair into a manageable, affable crew cut that betrays no hint of the chaos within its owner's mind.

2) With the help of Big Kenny, owner of the Old Wee Scotch Things Shop, Kampala, choose a fine Glengarry hat in traditional McAmin clan tartan.

3) Feed Big Kenny to the crocodiles when the hat doesn't fit, and instead . . .

4) Over-promote yourself with a British Army Field-Marshal's cap. Ah, that's better! Now festoon the hat (and matching army uniform) with military honours you never earned and go around pretending you're just a lovable buffoon, not a murdering, baby-eating psychopath. No one will guess, honest . . .

margaret (baroness) thatcher

Prime Minister of the United Kingdom, 1979–1990

Oh, Margaret, before you came along, Britain was a genteel little country sliding into a post-Empire sunset of beige sandwiches and bad breath. And when you shattered the glass ceiling which indicated that a mere woman couldn't (and perhaps shouldn't) run anything more complex than a knitting circle, your helmet-headed approach was admired the world over.

Except in Britain, of course, where ungrateful peasants who'd lost jobs, homes and communities dared challenge your monetary revolution, bleating loudly about their plight.

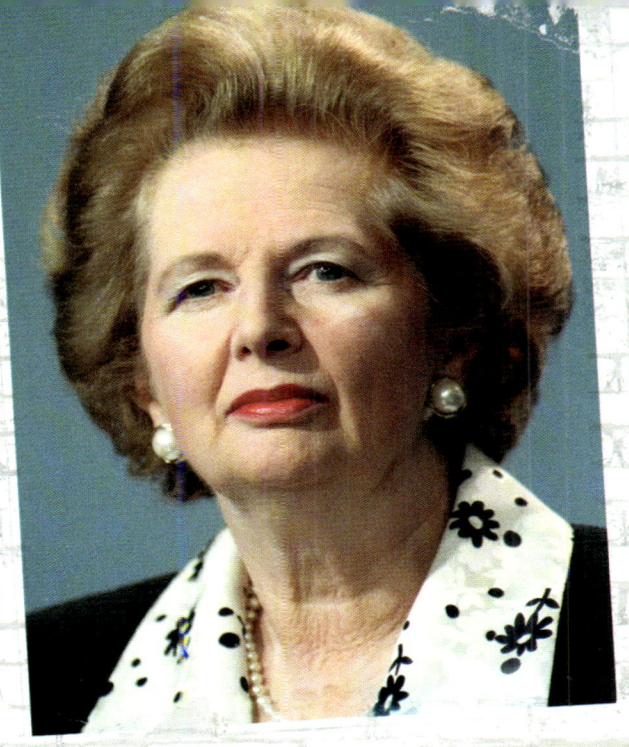

Luckily, your iconic golden halo deflected all the bombs, bullets and brickbats pesky Lefties and Argentinians could throw at it. 'You turn if you want to,' said The Thatch to those who said she was going too far, too fast, 'the Lady is not for turning.' And no wonder, when any sudden movement of that regal coiffure could severely threaten one's vertebrae.

Margaret's battle-worn 'do is a thing of beauty and influence, living on as it does in the stylings of Hillary Clinton, Marine Le Pen and, naturally, Donald Trump. In fact, some say that it is in fact *the same hair*, stolen from The Lady's body in the dead of night and shared among those who believe in going into a fight head first.

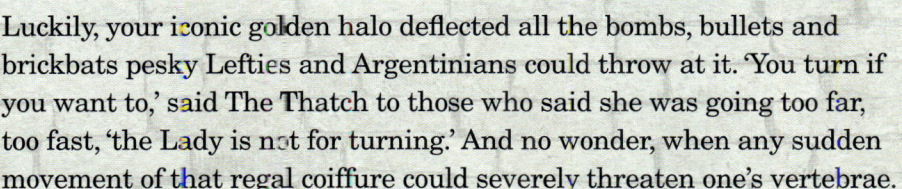

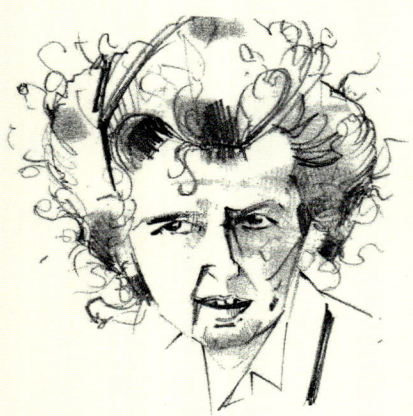
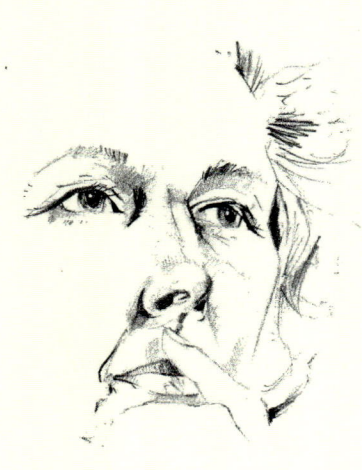

Straight Outta Valhalla for this battle maiden!

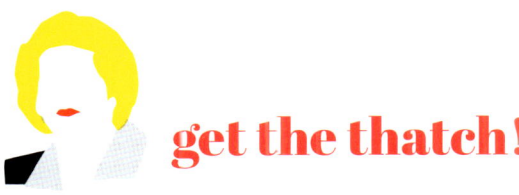

get the thatch!

1) Enter a hairdresser's in a small market town, privatise it immediately and demand the staff call you 'Ma'am' as they apply their idle hands to your tousled head.

2) Next, sit under a drier for at least an hour and gaze regally into the middle distance.

3) When the hair is adequately baked, test its resilience by firing an Exocet missile at it.

4) Finally, pick the shade you most wish to go into battle with. A steely hue of platinum – to match your supporters' credit cards – will do nicely.

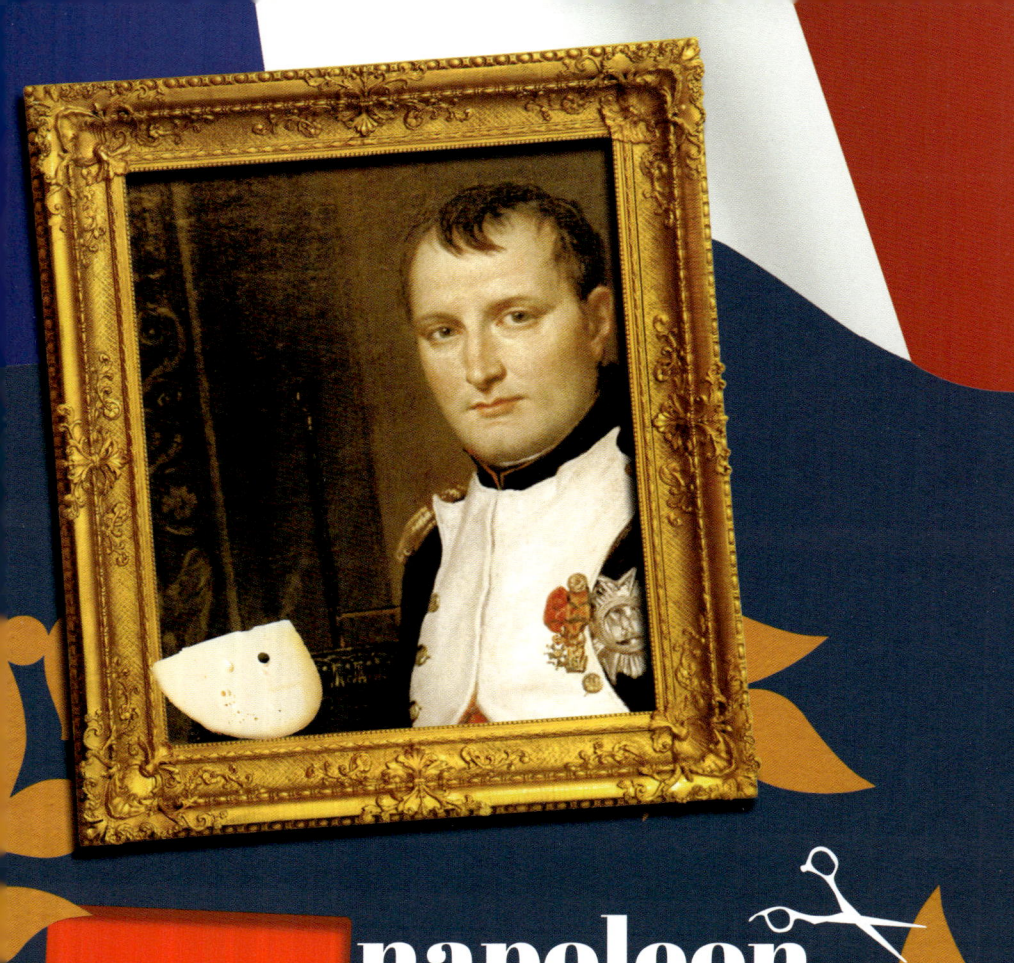

napoleon bonaparte

Emperor of the French, 1804–1821

Zut alors! There they were, lounging around in their fancy 'jardins publiques' with their mistresses and their cheese and wine, and next second the poor old French are retreating from Moscow and surviving on chilled rat. Oh, Nappy B, where did it all go wrong?!

In history, a badass tends to come along when life needs shaking up. In Boney's case, his imperial ambitions far outstripped the calls from his wife Josephine to make constant whoopee and grow corpulent on the best cuisine La Belle France had to offer. Instead, he dragged the poor peasantry out of their Beaujolais-induced slumbers and threw them at any army which defied him.

Success on the battlefield matched attitudes towards his own hair. From flyaway flibbertigibbet in his youth, Boney came to understand the power of a tight tonsure. Taking his cue from Ancient Rome, Nappy had a classic 'tongue and groove' cut (i.e. allowing a flap of hair to grow at the front in a rude gesture towards enemies) beloved by Caesar, Nero, etc.

By matching this with a crown of laurel leaves, Boney's 'little man syndrome' aspirations were complete. Even in exile, when he was Emperor of nowhere other than a nasty bit of rock, his hair still flicked in vulgar fashion towards his British captors. Intent on entertaining his wife and drinking his entire wine cellar, the lumpen Brits simply 'ne se souciait pas'.

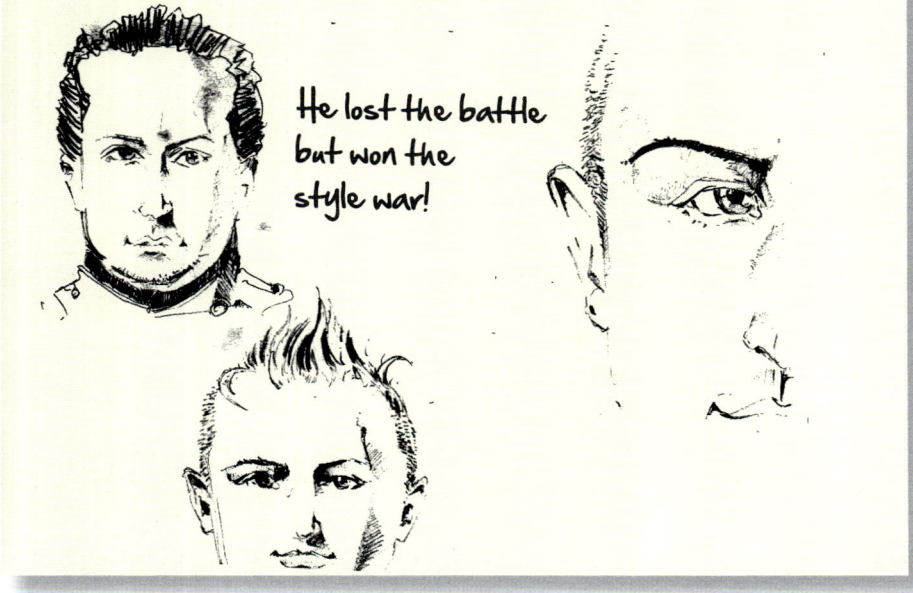

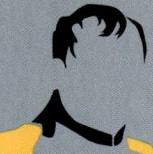# get the blown-aparte!

1) Take yourself seriously. Very, very seriously, and shave off those poetic locks.

2) Next, trim back the hair on the top of the head leaving a three-inch strip.

3) Flick this forwards in a semi-curl of arrogance towards your foes.

4) Stand on a rock in the middle of an ocean, alone, and shout: 'I am Napoleon Bonaparte! Look on my Works, ye Mighty, and despair!'

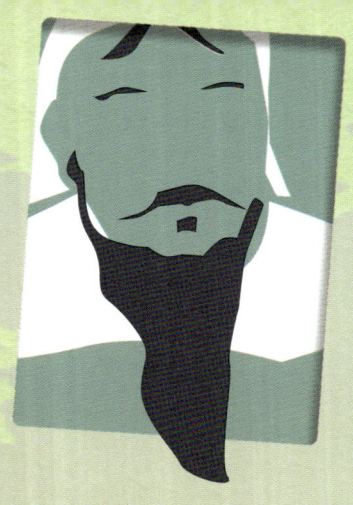

genghis khan

1st Great Khan of the Mongol Empire, 1206–1227

Spritually-enlightened leader of one of the world's greatest empires or genocidal maniac hell-bent on shaping the planet to his warped vision? Hey, it's not for a mere barber to decide – brothers, let's leave the politics in the playground, huh?

Suffice to say that Mr Khan was a guy who liked space around him – almost 10 million square miles, to be precise. Which is roughly how far his enemies wanted to be away from him, given his cut-throat reputation.

Yet he had this sensitive side, which can be seen in the few surviving portraits of him. The requisite villainous moustache, de rigeur among all homicidal dictators at the time, is offset by a rather grandfatherly grey beard. A deceptively gentle look is reminiscent of Bernie Sanders, despite the fact it gives him the appearance of a Shih Tzu with a bumble bee clinging to its anus.

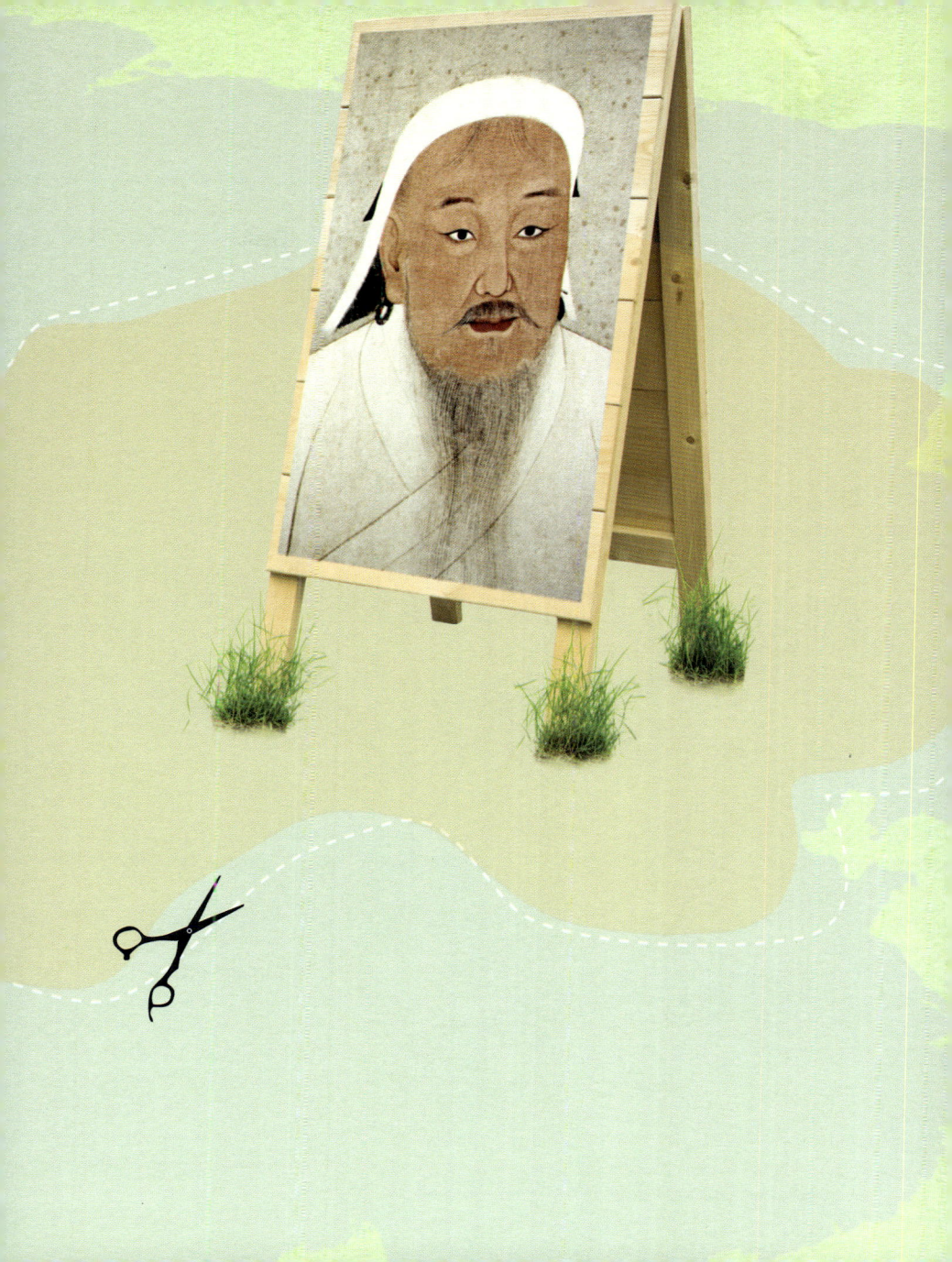

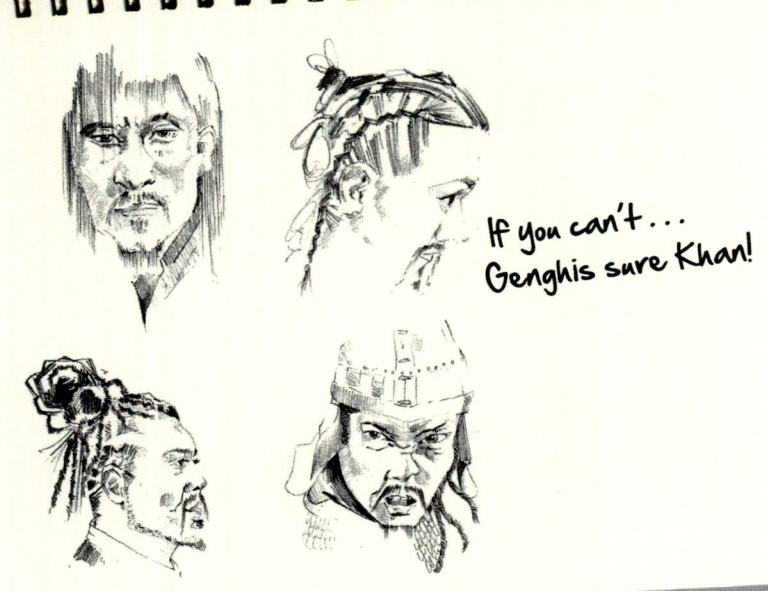

If you can't...
Genghis sure Khan!

get the geng-kiss!

1) First, get a little pasty around the chops. A certified organic yak- or sheep-fat foundation should do the trick.

2) Next, trim the moustache into the required shape and wax liberally at the ends, leaving a cruel disposition. A little braiding at the side of the head will not go amiss, either.

3) Tie up at the back and arrange the front of the hair into the 'lapping tongue' insult-cut (see The Blown-Aparte).

4) Trim and square the beard, highlighting it with shades of silver. Think annoying Tibetan lapdog.

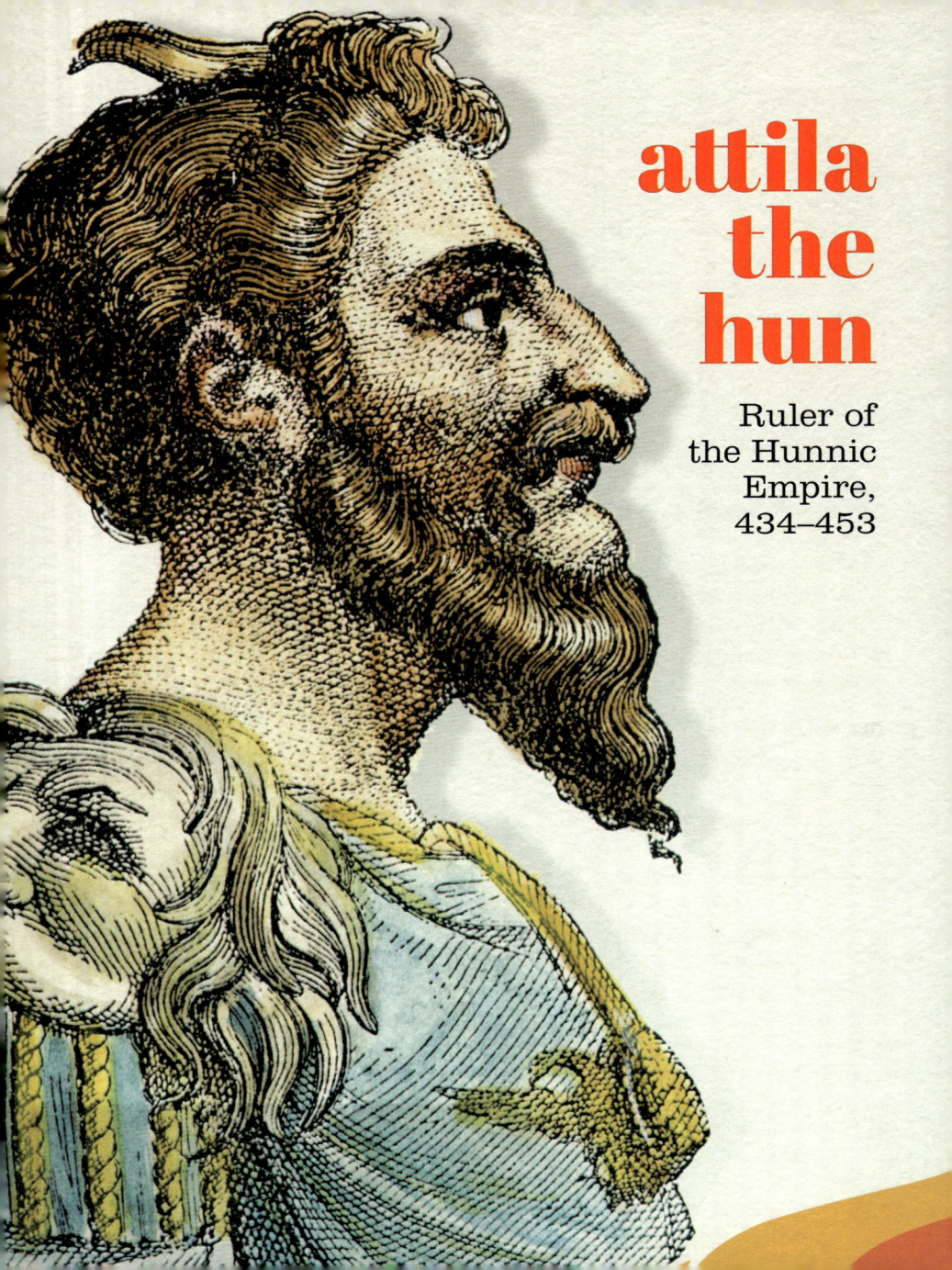

attila the hun

Ruler of the Hunnic Empire, 434–453

Here we go again – just when everything's rosy in the garden, along comes a giant poisonous weed snafu-ing everything in sight. Such is the case with Attila 'The Hun' Hun. Before his arrival, the Huns were a peaceable band of goat-traders, cultivating wild beetroot and growing their own sandals. Not the most exciting bunch on the planet, but nice all the same.

And afterwards, once Attila's eye-rolling and haughty way of marching drove equally peaceable tribes across Europe to their doom? Well, we had 'The Huns' – a race of efficient, moustachioed, spiky-helmeted and humourless übermensch bent on world domination. And boy, did they go to town on that idea in years to come . . .

Worst still, the Huns insisted on beating up the gentle Goths who were, of course, only interested in mooching about graveyards after midnight looking for vampires. But enough of the history lesson – what about the look? Naturally, it's classic villain territory: black hair sticking out of the sides of the helmet, Fu Manchu moustache, wild eyes, furry hat – come on, what's not to fear?!

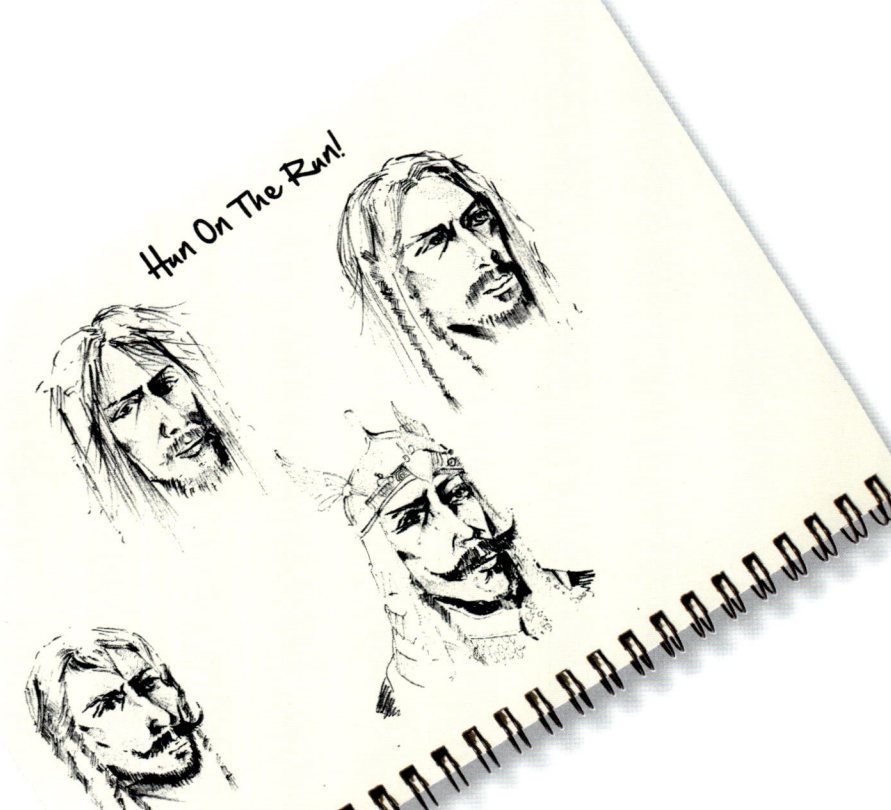

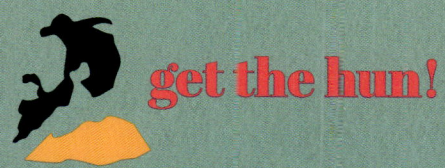

get the hun!

1) You're way too caveman – ruffle those feathers and go as rough as you like!

2) Stop shaving, start growing. The hair, the moustache, the pointy beard. The whole damn lot!

3) Practise your wild-eyed stare in the mirror, then turn it on your kids. Did they howl? Excellent!

4) Ramp up the terror with a spiky winged helmet, or a freshly skinned fur hat complete with dripping bloodstains.

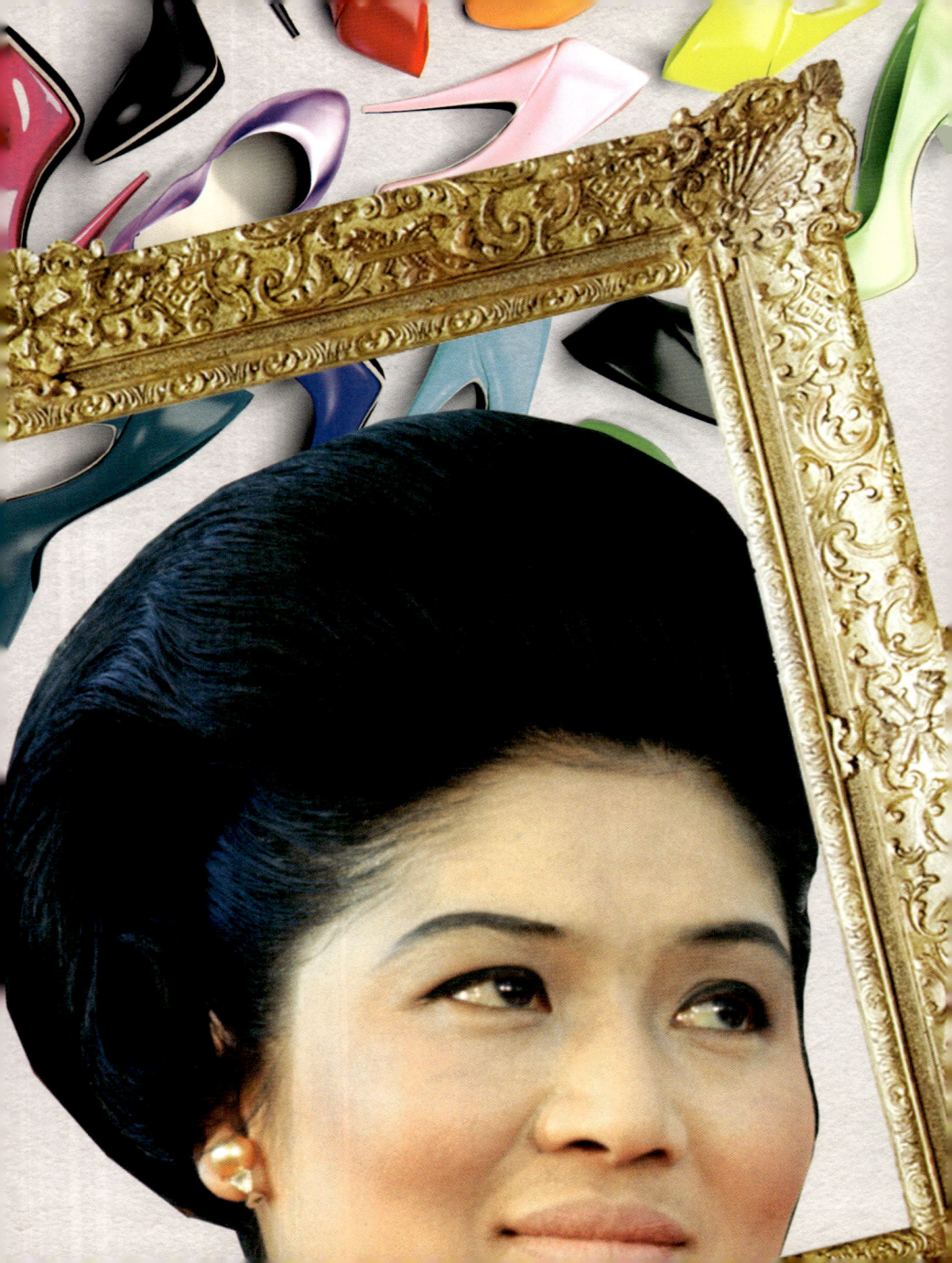

imelda marcos

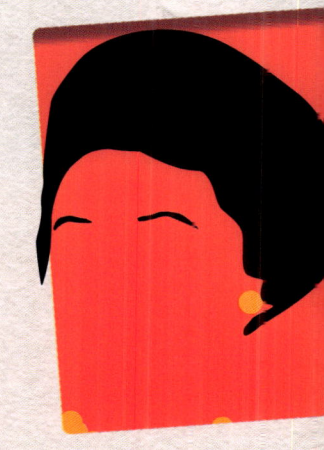

Widow of Ferdinand Marcos. 10th First Lady of the Philippines, 1965–1986

Gloriously ambitious and extravagant, Imelda Marcos is more famous for her shoes than her 'dos but in the days before she cleaned out every branch of Jimmy Choo the world over, Meldie sported a deadly black beehive that paid fitting tribute to the 'Elvis in Vegas' years.

And, best of all, she still does! At the time of writing, the 'Iron Butterfly' is heading towards her 90s and is still politicking all over the country, demanding respect and provoking controversy wherever she goes. Now in its tenth decade, the beehive has been officially recognised as a World Heritage Site, such is its spectacular construction and international architectural interest.

Woe betide anyone who suggests Meldie goes grey quietly. What's a few million on octopus ink to the lady who once spent $2,000 at an airport on chewing gum? Get real. She's sassy, classy and brassy, and in a world where tyrants' widows spend the rest of their lives increasingly resembling pot-bellied stoves, Meldie is a reminder that bad is a Thing, and not always a bad Thing . . .

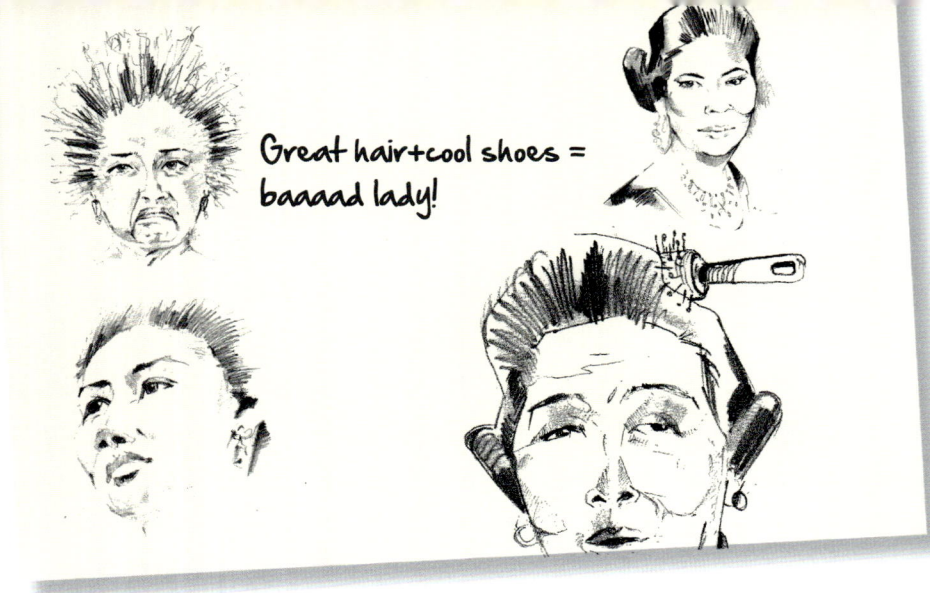

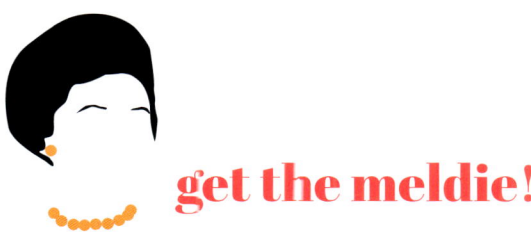

get the meldie!

1) Blacken the erratic hair with octopus ink (10 gallons) then spray the monthly equivalent of the Philippines' chemical manufacturing output liberally into it.

2) With a click of your fingers, order a 22-carat gold hairbrush made by the Fabergé company and tease the tresses into a beehive.

3) Gently remove any scaffolding from around the hair and check for structural cracks.

4) Call in UNESCO inspectors and declare the 'do an Ancient Monument.

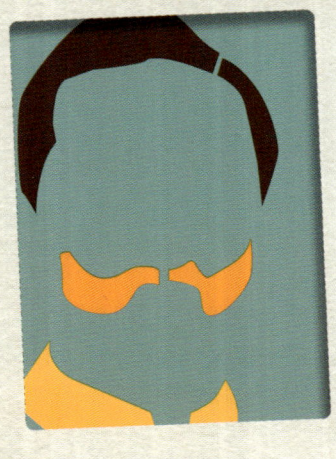

kaiser wilhelm II

German Emperor and King of Prussia, 1888–1918

As a grandson of Queen Victoria, Wilhelm, the future Emperor of Germany, would often be seen at the annual family holiday in Balmoral dressed in kilt and Glengarry. As with Idi Amin, the penchant for uniforms never quite left young Villy and, like most Germans, he only ever felt wholly comfortable in full military dress.

However, the disaster which befell Germany after the First World War (all Wilhelm's fault, natch) was nothing compared to what happened to him as a teenager. While bathing in a lake, Wilhelm was attacked by a migrating swallow which became stuck to his upper lip and, despite all efforts, could not be removed.

After months of torment, Wilhelm decided to accept his new companion and indeed, fashioned the design of his Imperial helmet upon a bird (albeit an eagle – the swallow was considered somewhat feminine). Yet its constant fluttering and twittering caused Wilhelm deep psychological difficulties, leading to quickness of temper and erratic decision-making. The rest, as they say, is history. Nice uniform, though . . .

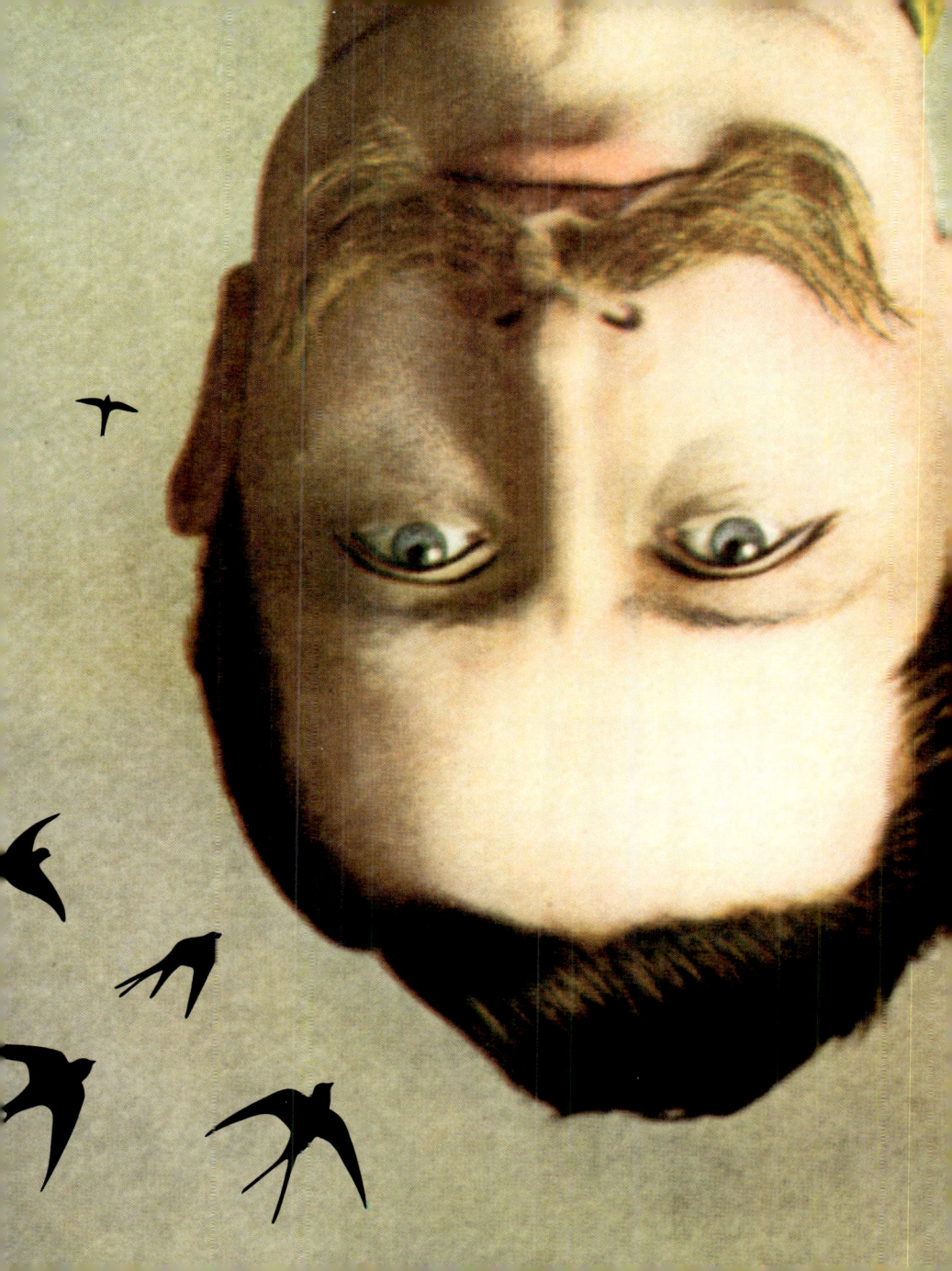

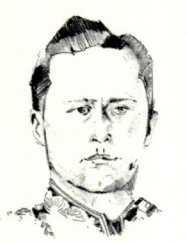
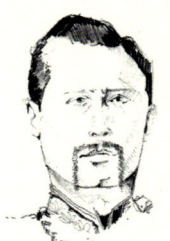
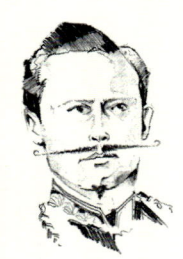
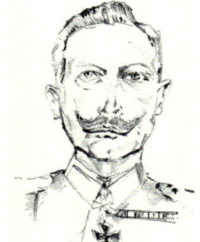

Ve haf ways of making you squawk!

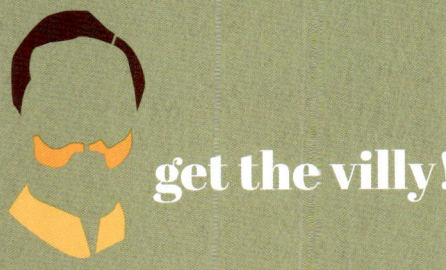

get the villy!

1) Undergo a razor-cut around the back and sides of the head in silent, Teutonic fashion.

2) Feel free to try different moustache styles including the Zapata and ...

3) ... the ridiculous Frenchman. Eventually, destiny will intervene when ...

4) ... a swallow will attach itself to your upper lip. Keep it there with industrial-strength epoxy resin and award oneself the Iron Cross for valour.

manuel noriega

Military Dictator of Panama, 1983–1989

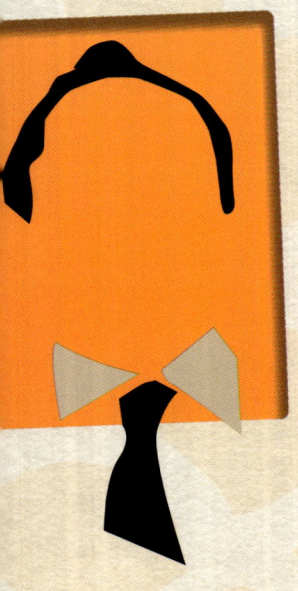

Pock-marked Panamanian nasty Manuel Noriega missed a golden opportunity to become President for Life. Instead, he lasted just six years, and all because of bad hair advice. Years collaborating with the CIA gave him an air of invincibility – but what he didn't realise was that tastes change and by the late 1980s he was yesterday's man.

This wasn't because he'd stretched the Americans' patience with his blatant drug trafficking. It was because he point-blank refused to go all late-80s 'Big Hair'. Had he done so, the course of his Hairstory would've been so different.

Known among his people as Old Pineapple Face, Nori's locks should've embraced his nickname. Had he asked, The Brush would've advised him on a stylish arrangement of woven blonde dreads and extensions sticking through a cherry-red bandana, reflecting his famous moniker. Little children would've

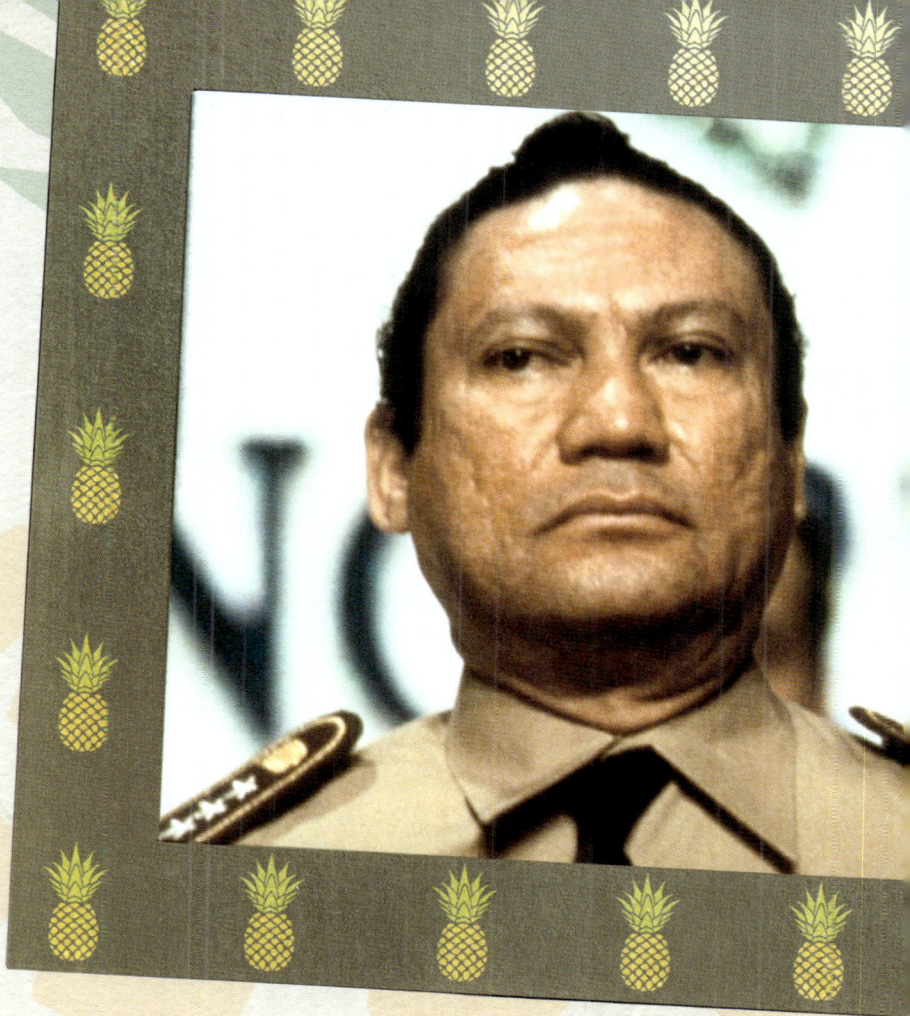

danced through the streets of Panama City and the CIA would've departed for good.

But no. He stuck with his dull cut and ended up hiding in a shower block, psyched out by US Marines playing endless loops of Guns N' Roses albums. See what happens when you don't listen to your barber . . . ?

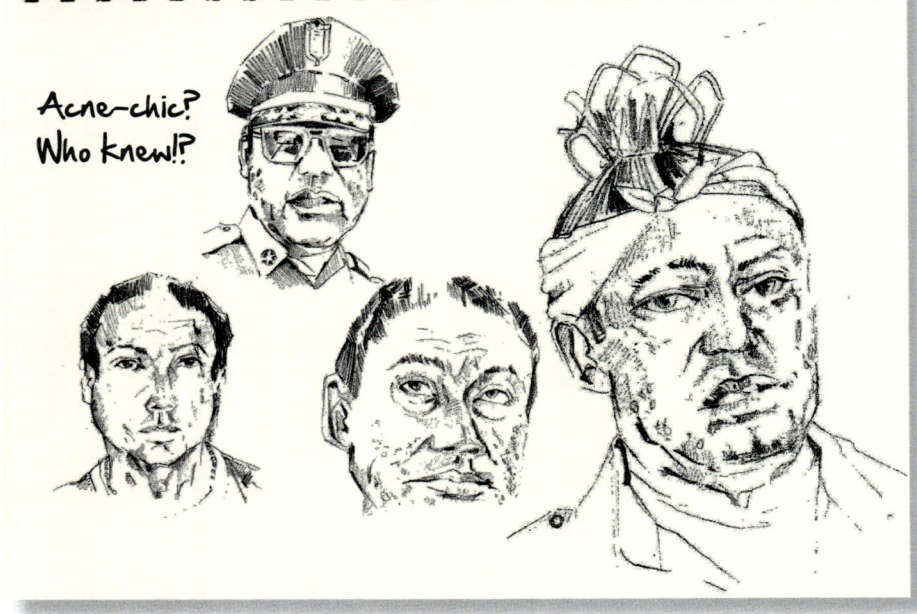

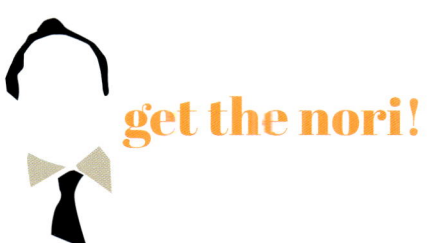

get the nori!

1) You're plain ugly and look like a pineapple. So ask your barber for some great advice!

2) Allow the expert to weave in a winning combo of woven dreads and extensions. Surf's up, Nori!

3) Tie up with an 'I'm With The CIA!' logo bandana.

4) Go as metal as you like – Metallica, Slayer, Aerosmith, Motorhead: those army dudes will never winkle you out of your mosh pit!

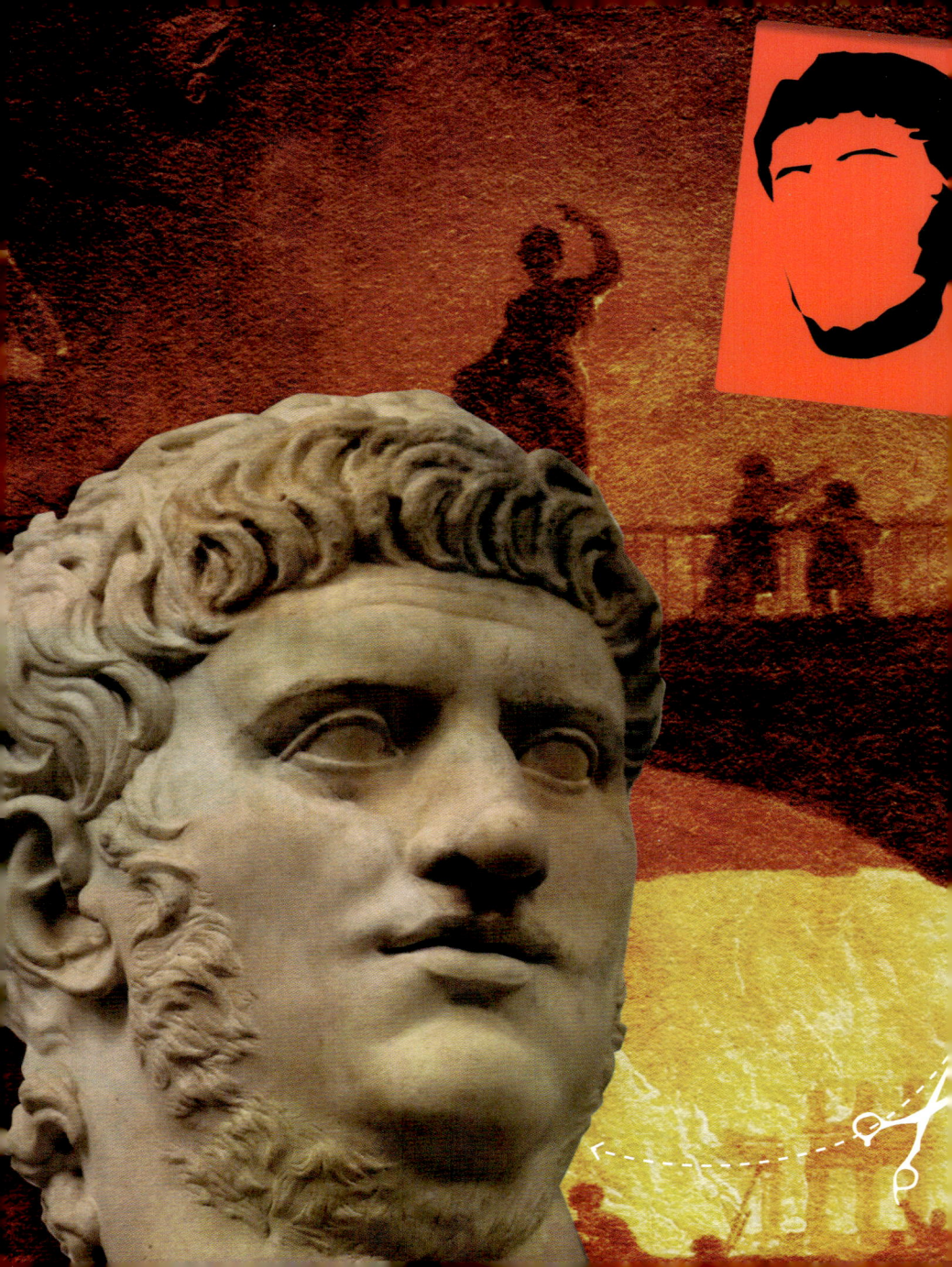

nero claudius caesar augustus germanicus

5th Emperor of the Roman Empire, 64AD–68AD

Well, lookee here! Mommy-murdering musician Nero might have been as mad as a fried squirrel, but somehow he bequeathed his distinctive chinstrap beard to no less sober a set of folk as the Amish. Who knew!?

It's true. When he wasn't castrating boys and then marrying them, culture-vulture Nero slipped into pastoral mode, cultivating a humble shepherd's beard and playing the fiddle for the entertainment and pleasure of his subjects.

This rural idyll couldn't last forever. Rome burning down in 64AD wasn't quite the distraction from his spendthrift economic policy Nero had hoped for. Nevertheless, a mass crucifixion of Christians soon appeased the smokin' Romans and order was restored.

His suicide in 68AD might have been the end of it, but style isn't forgotten quickly. And in a curious twist of Hairstory, the chinstrap became a favourite of animal-loving peaceniks, pipe-smokers, left-wing politicians, Methodists and Amish. Go figure . . . ?

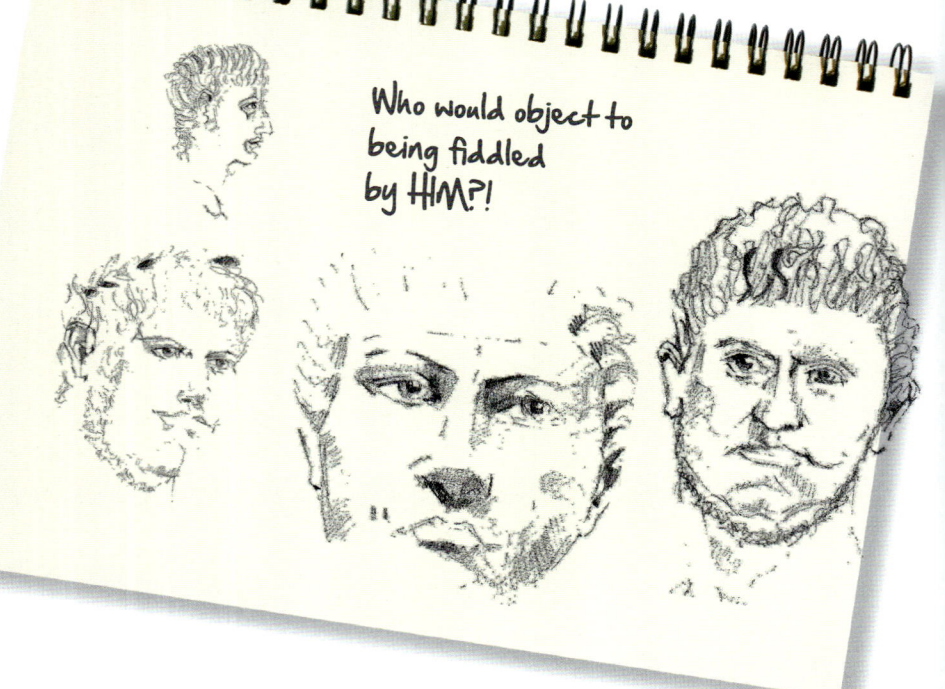

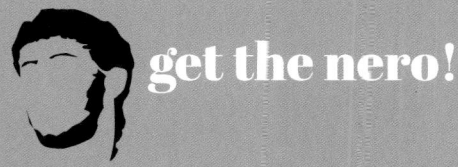# get the nero!

1) Play the fiddle? Got welts on your neck caused by constant violin practice? Then . . .

2) Grow a protective chinstrap!

3) Cultivate complementary curly locks and crown with laurels.

4) Disguise yourself as the Empress and marry a eunuch!

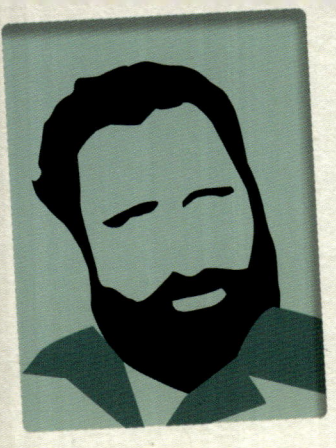

fidel castro

17th President of Cuba, 1976–2008

The verdict of history splits 50/50 in the case of the late Fidel Castro, former President of Cuba. Good guy? Bad guy? Cigar-loving socialist granddaddy or Commie of the Caribbean? Ah, who cares – as ever, it's his Hairstory he'll be remembered for, not how many banana collectives he visited.

As we know, never changing your look is a double-edged scissor – you're kind of stuck in the past and yet, you never seem to grow older. Sometime in the early 50s Fidel's bromance with hotster guerilla Che Guevara turned copycat, as Fidel took a piece of those poster-boy curly locks 'n' beard combo for himself.

Sadly, dumpy Fidel was no looker and, unlike Che, had no chance of ever having a beautiful corpse. So he did the next best thing by taking the advice of the Havana Women's Revolutionary Fashion Polizia, going for an all-over green colour scheme, keeping the beard and topping out with a 'hasta la revolución!' military cap.

And wow, did that look catch on! Limp-wristed socialist vegetarian males everywhere got the face-fuzz 'n' fatigues combo, and discovered a sisterhood more than willing to chow down on a late-night Cohiba! And not a tractor factory in sight!

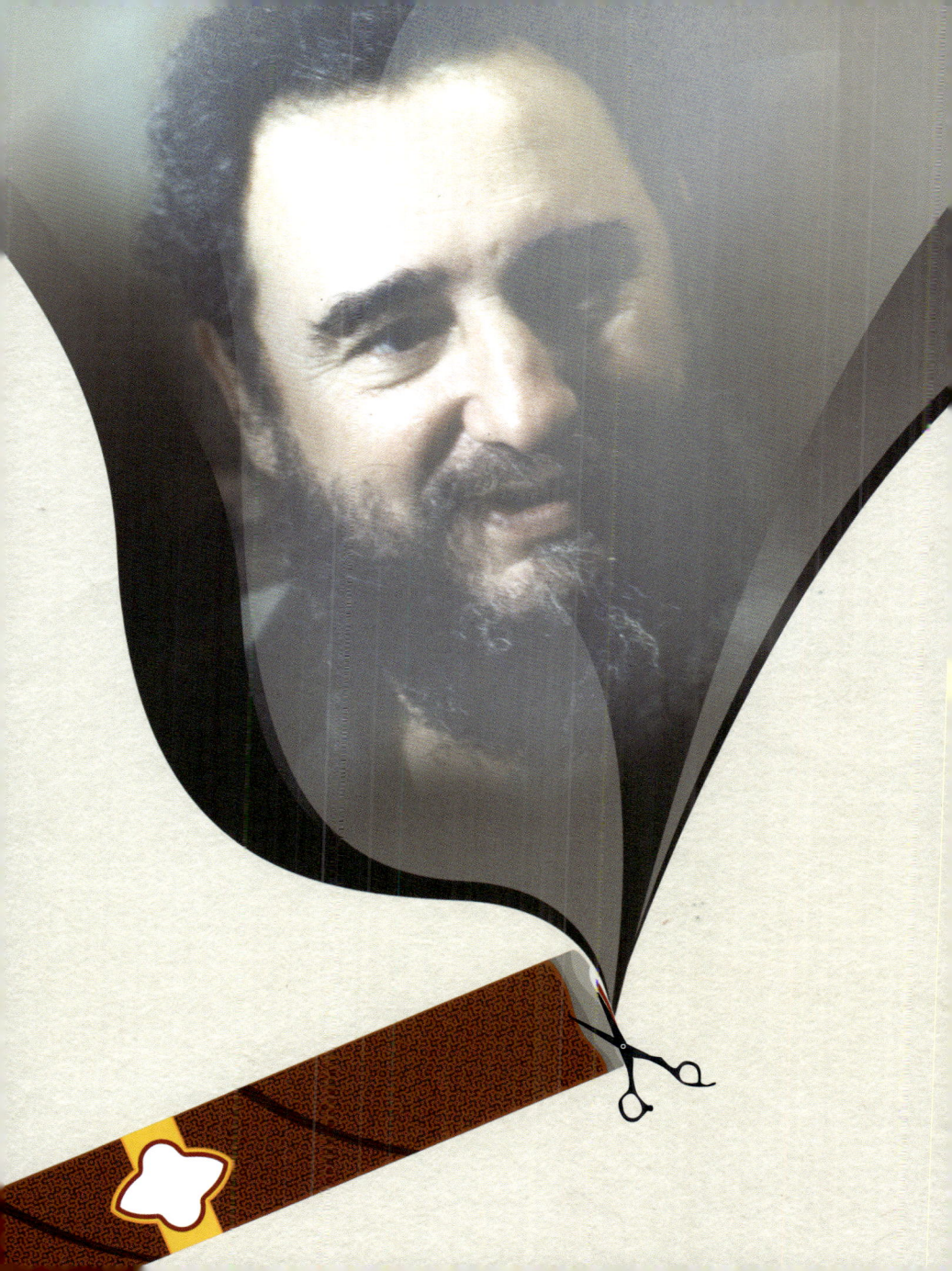

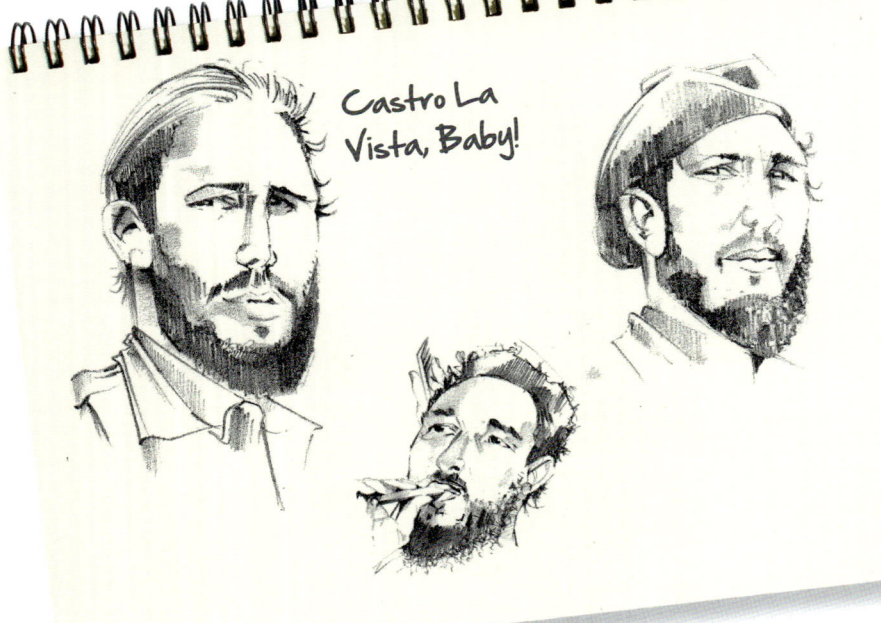

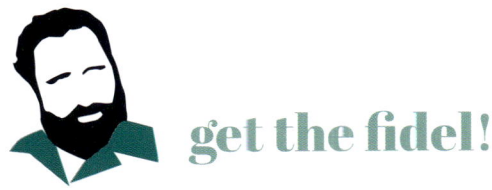

get the fidel!

1) Face facts, fat-face: you'll never be Che Guevara. So lose the beret ASAP.

2) Start smoking hand-rolled Cuban cigars, especially when threatened with nuclear annihilation.

3) The beard isn't coming entirely naturally (in fact, it looks like a deserted owl's nest) but keep at it because . . .

4) One day it will outlive every Commie pinko leader in history!

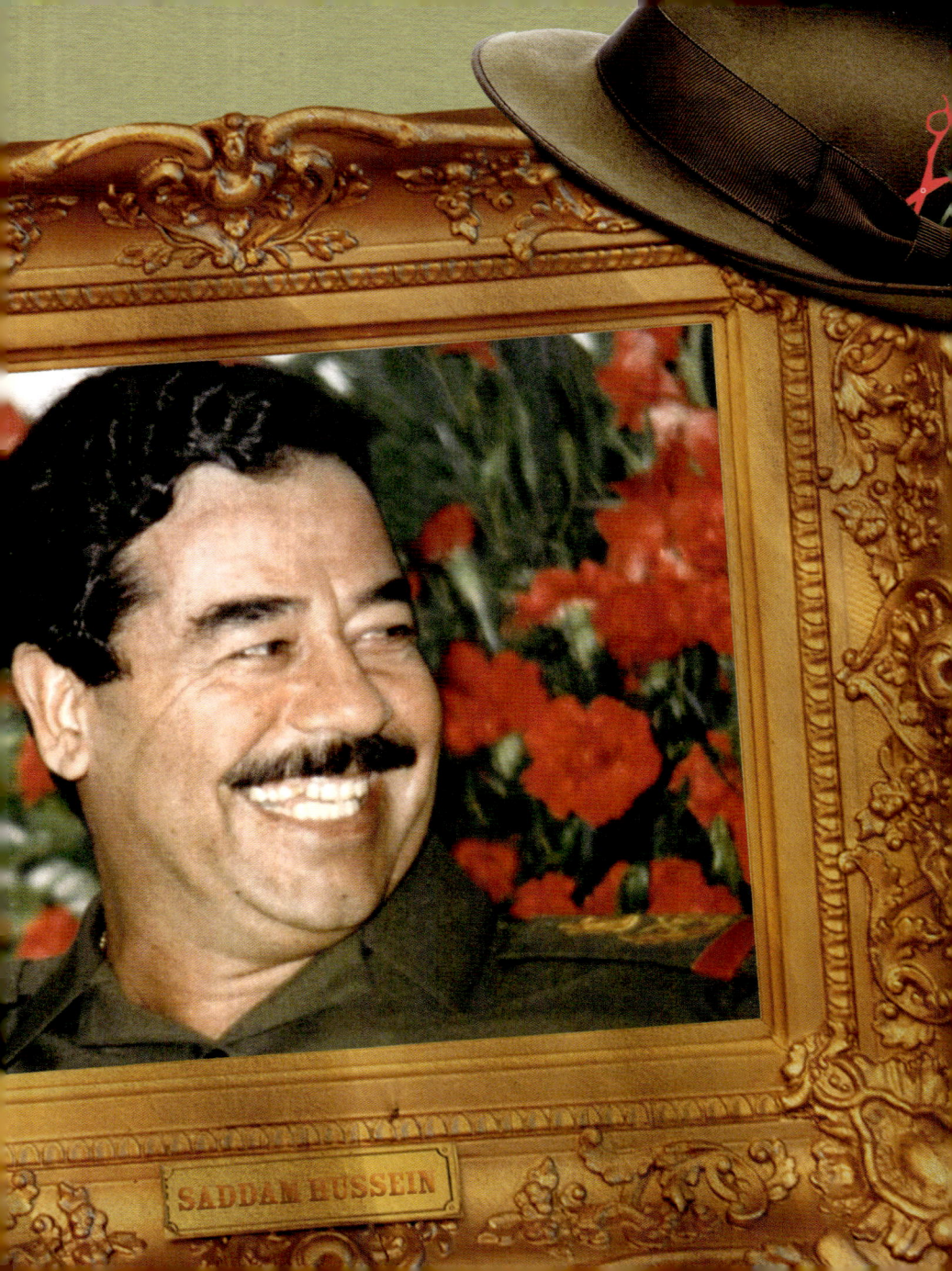

saddam hussein

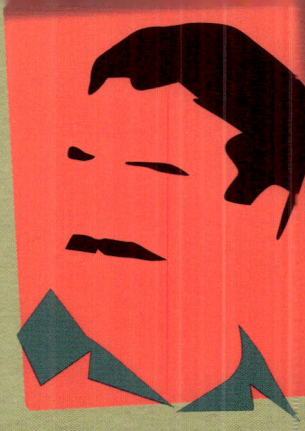

5th President of Iraq, 1979–2003

Oh Sadders . . . didn't you learn anything at Despot School? Not least about subterfuge, and the whole good cop/bad cop thing? Obviously not, which is why you ended up hiding in a storm drain in your knickers.

There comes a point where fooling the public in order to secure a solid dictatorial future for yourself and your murderous sons means you need to box clever. So don't – I repeat, DON'T – sweep your dastardly black hair back into a bouffant and don't, on any account, get a similarly hued moustache.

Equally, divert your eyes away from that sinister black beret you spotted in the casbah. How about a nice Homburg instead? Oh, you tried that . . . and you STILL look like a swivel-eyed baby-eater. Bad luck, man.

Interestingly enough, Sadders's finest fashion moment came during his trial. With his 'I'm-Really-Not-Him, Honest' beard newly trimmed, and sporting a nice suit and tieless shirt, Sadd's sartorial sharpness was a snip off the old Yves Saint Laurent block. Unfortunately it didn't save him from the gallows, but still . . . he went in style.

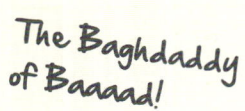
The Baghdaddy of Baaaad!
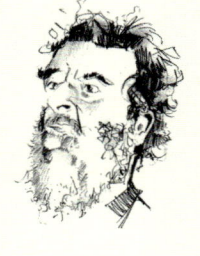
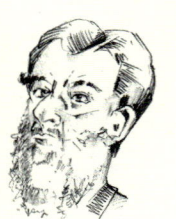
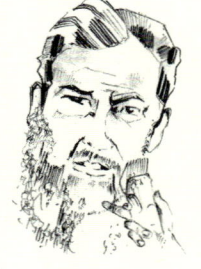
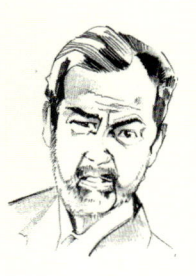

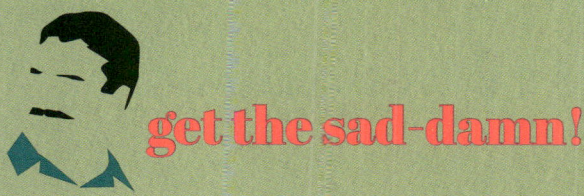
get the sad-damn!

1) Watch six back-to-back episodes of Hanna-Barbera's *Wacky Races* and imagine Dick Dastardly's moustache attached to Mutley the dog's top lip. Great, we're getting somewhere now, but you're still a little shaggy, so . . .

2) Sweep back that hair with my own brand Desert Delight hair product until it resembles a blown oil well.

3) Thicken the moustache to evil sea-slug proportions and get rid of extraneous face-fuzz.

4) Facing the Grim Reaper? Go out in style, with Savile Row suit and gentlemanly salt-and-pepper beard.

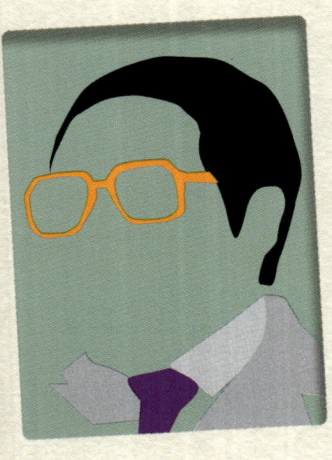

robert mugabe

President of Zimbabwe, 1980–present

A h, good morning Mr Mugabe . . . your usual short-back-and-sides? Sit right down in the chair and make yourself comfortable, old boy. Magazine? Yes, I think we have the latest *Tyrant's Weekly* somewhere . . . oh, and you want your moustache trimmed too? That's fine, but you know, Bobby, I've been meaning to have a word with you about that. Listen up for a moment . . .

You've heard of Adolf Hitler, right? Yes, he was a bad guy. A very bad guy. And you're a pretty bad guy too. Why thank you, you're most welcome. And yes, you both share a cute little Charlie Chaplin moustache. Except that Herr Hitler wasn't basing his look on the celebrated cinema great . . . and I don't think you are either, are you?

The thing is, Bobby, no matter how much you admire his leadership style, there's no getting away from the fact that Hitler was a racist. He wasn't keen on anyone not from northern Europe, and certainly not anyone who wasn't white. Do you see what I'm getting at, Bobby? There's a big difference between you and him. Just look at the pictures, and tell me what it is.

Oh, I get it! You're a racist too! You chased most of the whites from your country? Well keep going, keep growing, is what I say. If you want to look like the most evil man in history, go right ahead. That little toothbrush effect suits you down to the ground. And that'll be $200 for the trim and another $50 for the advice. Goodbye!

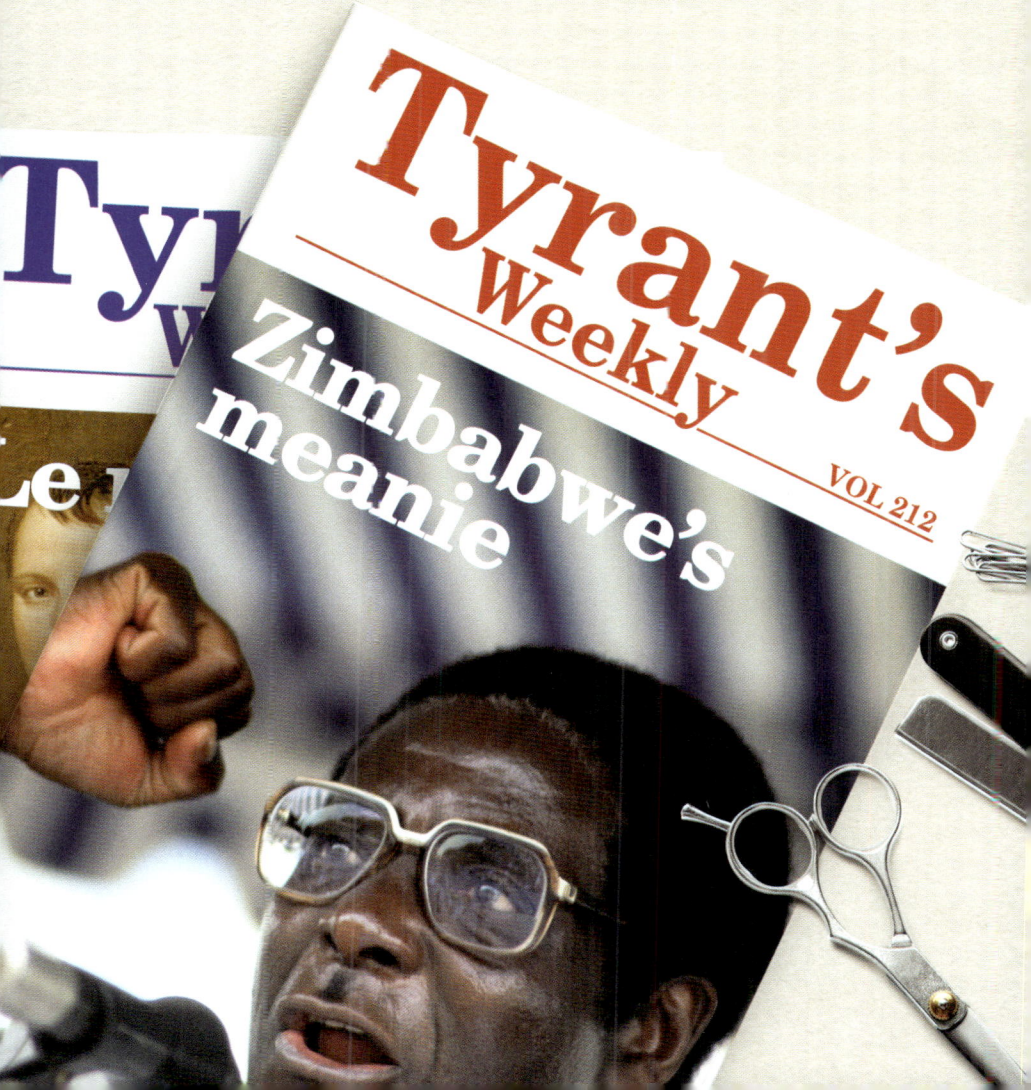

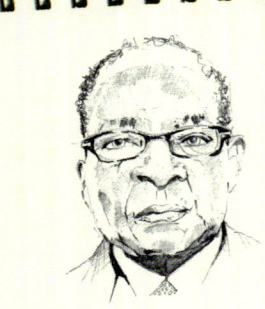
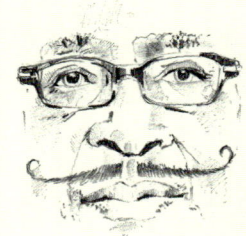

Rockin' Robert – the toothbrush 'tashe revival starts here!

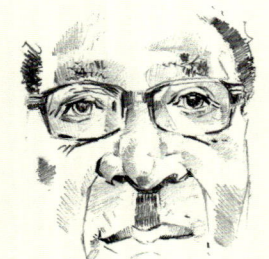
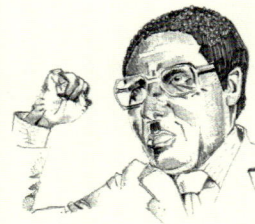

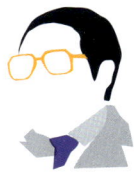

get the mug-abe

1) Keep the hair nice and close-cropped. The mouth is where all the politics comes from, not out of the top of your head (usually), so keep the focus below eye-level.

2) You have a pronounced philtrum (that dinky little groove from below your nose to your top lip). Cool! So let's plug that gap with . . . a Hercule Poirot 'tache?

3) NO! A Hitler moustache! Not too big, but enough to say, 'Look who's boss.'

4) A pair of 1970s CBS news anchor's glasses tops out the look perfectly. The 'black Adolf' never looked so swish.

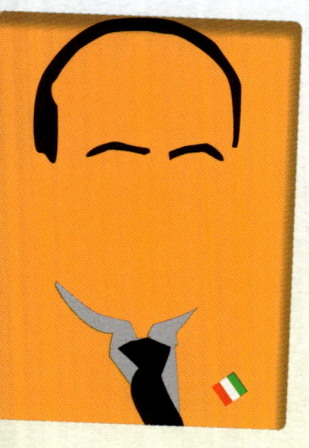

benito mussolini

27th Prime Minister of Italy, 1922–1943

Hapless neo-Roman emperor and boot-licking Hitler toadie Benito Mussolini sure made Italians step in line and the trains run on time, and all thanks to his famous 'baldylocks' 'do.

The archetypal shaven-headed fascist thug, Benny gave pitiable, lonely and balding men everywhere the opportunity to blame their sexual inadequacies on various minorities. Combine the look with a proud, prominent jawline and a hands-on-hips stance, and we have the epitome of the strutting 1930s bully-boy.

It wasn't to last. Benny's Hairstory went all kaput when he got into bed with Adders Hitler (not literally – or so we're told . . .). Busy tending olive groves and winking at pretty girls, most Italian men didn't want anything approaching a war but unfortunately they got one. And how. By 1943 Musso's days were up, and never again would the early-morning scrape of razor against bonce be heard around Rome's Piazza Venezia.

Finally he was caught, shot by his own side and strung up from the roof of a gas station. That said, even hanging upside down there was still no chance of a bad hair day for Benny . . .

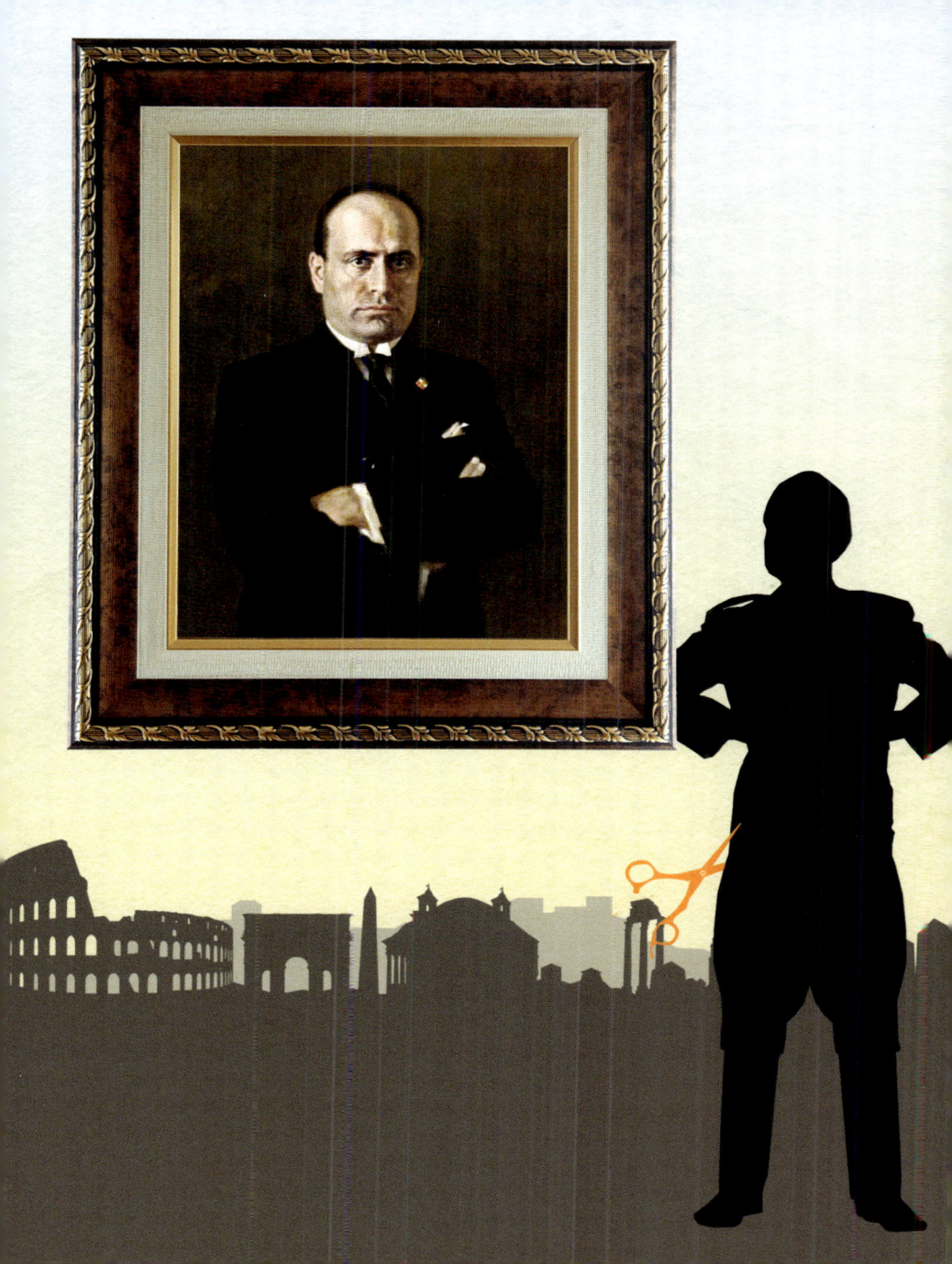

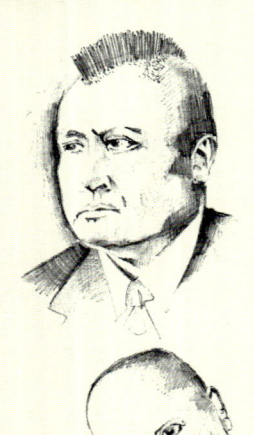
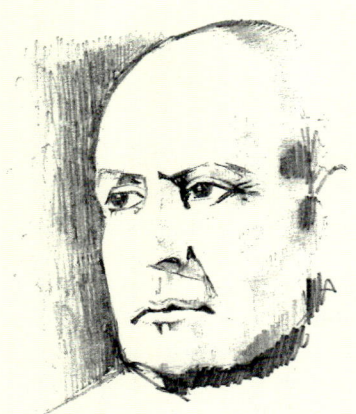
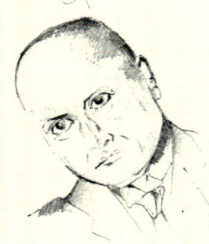

In any ristorante he'd be dish of the day!

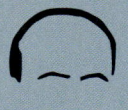

get the muscle-ini!

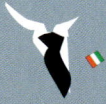

1) Lose, lose, lose the hair! Bald men have virility, style and power (say the wives of bald men) so lose the locks and keep the looks! And no, don't leave a 'fun' Mohawk . . . it's not clever.

2) Razor-cut every day to achieve Turbo-Power Virility level.

3) Work on the jutting jaw and baleful stare . . .

4) Try practising hanging upside down every day. Not only does it make you virile and clever, you never know when it might come in handy . . .

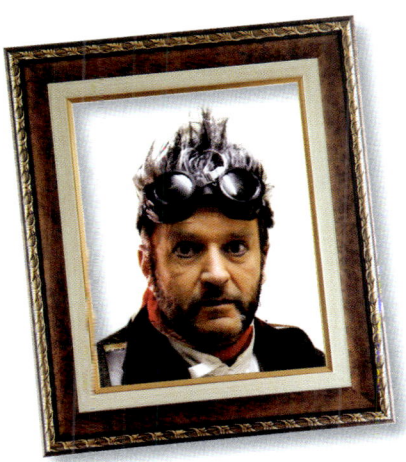

the author

The book is curated by celebrity hairstylist Bryan 'The Brush' Burnsides. Bryan was born Morag McNeish in Paisley, Scotland, but moved away at the first sign of rain. A transitioning female-to-hipster and a former Miss Scissors Scotland (1993, Expat Category), Bryan is currently official Ponytail Consultant at the Squatting Beaver Indian Reservation, South Dakota.

the author's friend

Cut It Out is ably co-authored by British writer Tom Henry who, among other worthy publications, assisted with 2016's *The Turnip Prize – A Retrospective* (an academically comprehensive guide to the best of the world's worst art) and, at the age of 50, has a surprisingly fulsome head of hair, most of which is his.

the illustrator

Jed Rouncefield Franklin is a contemporary figurative artist. He studied Fine Art in Bristol and has shown his work internationally. Jed lives and works in the South West of England and splits his time between being a studio artist and a teacher.

Jed is passionate about painting and drawing people, capturing their unique personality and their real world interactions.

Photo credits – Kim Jong-un: Xinhua News Agency/REX/Shutterstock; Grigori Rasputin: Apic/Getty Images; Muammar Gaddafi: AGF s.r.l./REX/Shutterstock; Donald Trump: Andrew Milligan/PA Archive/PA Images; Adolf Hitler: Roger Viollet/Getty Images; Josef Stalin: akg-images; Mao Tse-tung: Sipa Press/REX/Shutterstock; Idi Amin Dada: Allstar Picture Library/Alamy Stock Photo; Margaret Thatcher: Allstar Picture Library/Alamy Stock Photo; Napoleon Bonaparte: Pictorial Press Ltd/Alamy Stock Photo; Genghis Khan: Granger Historical Picture Archive/Alamy Stock Photo; Attila the Hun: Granger/REX/Shutterstock; Imelda Marcos: Bettmann/Getty Images; Kaiser Wilhelm: Lordprice Collection/Alamy Stock Photo; Manuel Noriega: Sipa Press/REX/Shutterstock; Nero: Lanmas/Alamy Stock Photo; Fidel Castro: nikwheeler/Alamy Stock Photo; Saddam Hussein: Sipa Press/REX/Shutterstock; Robert Mugabe: Bettmann/Getty Images; Benito Mussolini: Chronicle/Alamy Stock Photo; Scottish Terrier: Linn Currie/Shutterstock ; wooden sign board: VTT Studio/Shutterstock ; swarm of bats: Reinke Fox/Shutterstock; grass: Fotoslaz/Shutterstock; cheese: Maffi/Shutterstock; birds: GooseFrol/Shutterstock; pineapples: Syquallo/Shutterstock; coal pile: Chatchawal Kittirojana/Shutterstock; chair: arrogant/Shutterstock; gold laurel: dimair/Shutterstock; New York skyline: Greens87/Shuttertock; iron icon: berkut/Shutterstock; gold crown: Denis Rozhnovsky/Shutterstock; old poster background: Café Racer/Shutterstock; shoes: nuliplus/Shutterstock; gold: Jetchana wangkheeree/Shutterstock; various picture frames: Iakov Filimonov/Shutterstock; flags of the world: Thitipat Vatanasirithum/Shutterstock; notebook: puttography/Shutterstock; desert sand: juansanchez/Shutterstock; hat: Milos Luzanin; carnations: Igor Vkv/Shutterstock; barber shop equipment: Africa Studio/Shutterstock; Rome: josep perianes jorba/Shutterstock; Mao Tse-tung background: pixabay.com; *The Fire of Rome*, Hubert Robert (1785): Wikipedia; cigar: LVAconcept/Shutterstock

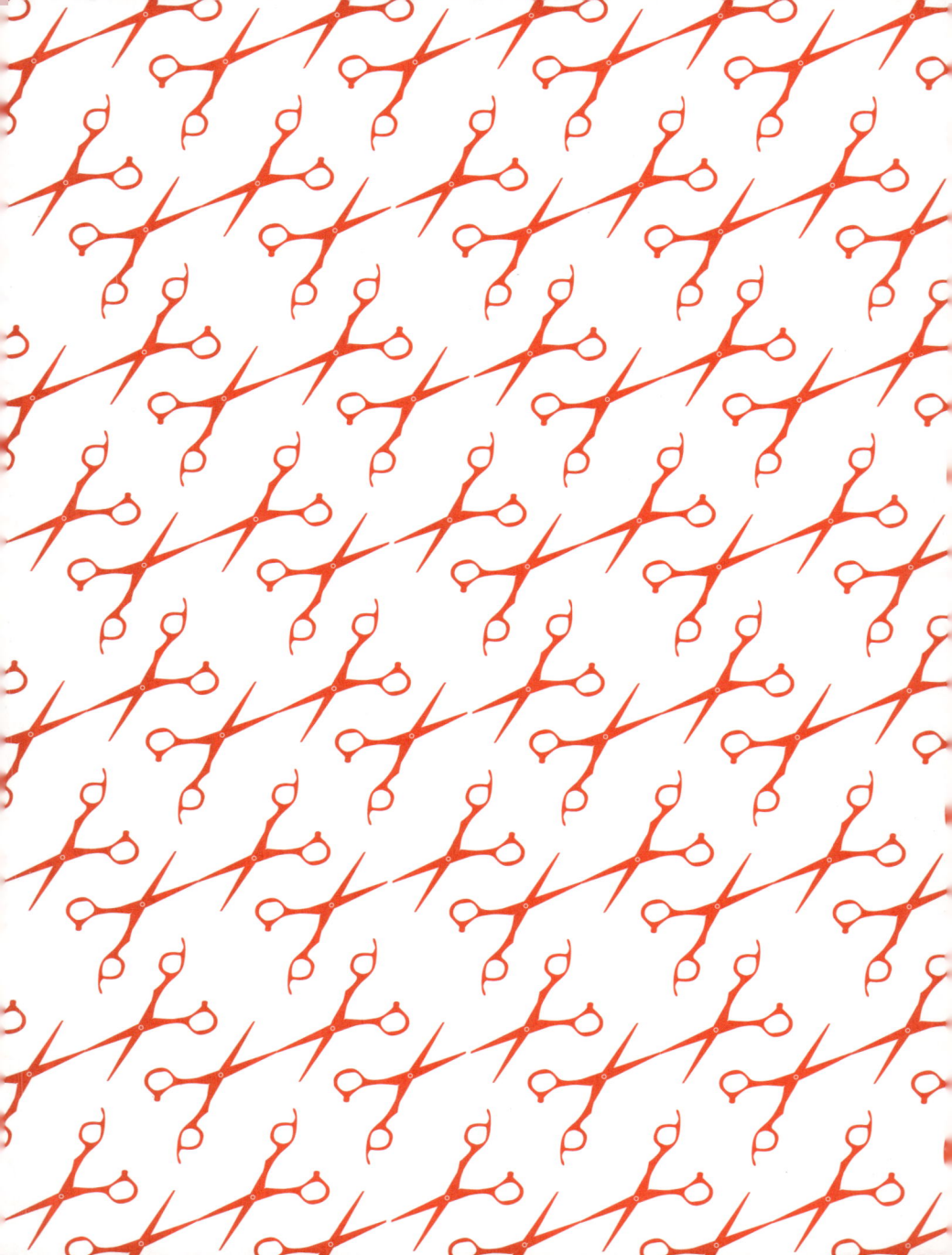